Great Monologues
for Young Actors

. . .

VOLUME II

For
Barbara Guile
and
Rick Bowen

Great Monologues
for Young Actors

. . .

VOLUME II

Edited by
Craig Slaight and Jack Sharrar

YOUNG ACTORS SERIES

A Smith and Kraus Book

A Smith and Kraus Book
Published by Smith and Kraus, Inc.
PO Box 127, Lyme, NH 03768

First Edition: February 1999
10 9 8 7 6 5 4

The Library of Congress Cataloging-In-Publication Data

Prepared by Quality Books Inc.

Great monologues for young actors vol.2 / [edited by] Craig Slaight and Jack Sharrar
p. cm. Includes bibliographical references.
ISBN 1-57525-106-X
1. Monologues. 2. Acting—Study and teaching.
I. Slaight, Craig, 1951– II. Sharrar, Jack, 1949–

PN4305.M6G4 1992 808.8245
QBI92-316

Contents

• • •

Monologues for Young Men

Introduction

• • •

Why should a book of monologues find its way into the hands of young actors? Isn't acting something that requires more than one ("duo")? What is the benefit of solo work in a collaborative art form? Shouldn't actors really concern themselves with complete plays in study and in work? These are all good questions, questions that are frequently asked by actors and critics of acting. Since what is before you is not only a book of monologues, but a second volume designed for the young actor, let us look for some possible answers.

The "monologue" has undergone many different uses over many years. Simply defined, a monologue is a speech from a play. The monologue is frequently seen as a solo or private scene. For the most part this isn't the case at all. Monologues are usually speeches from a larger scene, given by one character to another character(s) on stage at the time, and meant to further the forward action of the play and the objectives of the character speaking. In some cases the other character(s) is the audience—the character making a direct address to the theater audience, offering insight, clarification, narrative bridge, or in the case of some one-character plays, the communication of the life story of the character (i.e., *The Belle of Amherst, Mambo Mouth, Full Gallop*). In Shakespeare's plays, frequently the solo moment—or soliloquy—is a speech to oneself, the internal grappling of character obstacles in an external form (i.e., Hamlet's "To be, or not to be..."). In all cases, however, there is someone else present, even when that someone else is in fact the character's own conscience.

When the speech is isolated, particularly in an audition setting, we see and hear only one (mono) actor, but we are still having a *duo* experience in the character's life and within the context of a complete play. Without argument, the word *monologue* has become such a standard word in our theater vocabulary that when we use the word in the most basic the-ater setting we understand that it is a speech from a play, given by one actor.

In years now gone by, actors would be asked to audition for parts in plays by actually doing a scene from the play. Frequently the stage manager served as the "other" actor (even when the suitability of the stage manager to the role being read was anything but perfect). Although the producer or director focused their attentions on the actor vying for the role, what was seen was in fact a dialogue—sometimes con-taining a long speech. In today's theater world (even in the television and film industry) such "readings" are still pre-ferred, but something has been added before the actor actu-ally gets the opportunity of a scene reading. With the overwhelming army of actors vying for parts, an intricate audition structure has been erected. This process is the weed-ing out and the narrowing down of the clamoring throngs, to the final few that are the most potentially castable. During the important weeding out period, the required audition almost always involves the request for a "monologue." Countless solo auditions are conducted in this country every day, and it isn't just the professional world that holds such solo auditions. At this point in time the monologue is used as a judging measure for schools, colleges, universities, conser-vatories, youth theaters, community theaters, and the dreaded "contest." In fact, some groups are resorting to hav-ing the actor "put the monologue on videotape and mail it in" to constitute the audition, taking the process one step further away from human interaction. We could write pages here about the advantages of NOT using such an instrument to measure something as essential as the actor's ability. The two-minutes-or-bust mentality is certainly a less-than-perfect evaluation of the talents of an actor. As individual directors and teachers, we can choose not to use the solo audition in our process. However, with the many actors seeking the acting "experience" (be it amateur, school, or professional) and the ability to accommodate fewer than many, we see little change in the immediate future.

Here we offer monologues that *might* be suitable for a given audition. You will find a variety of characters, situations, and writing styles within this volume. But there is another place in your actor life where this monologue work can be incorporated: your training. If you only worked on monologues—without the other character present—you would have a totally inadequate preparation as an actor. Acting always involves someone else, even if that someone else is your alter ego, as in the soliloquy. Working only on isolated speeches from plays will be limiting and finally not fulfilling. We need to work with others to explore and grow. However, just as the musician works on solo pieces of music to stretch and sharpen techniques that serve their craft—and ultimately makes them stronger when playing with the orchestra—the actor most certainly can gain from exploring a character in smaller solo moments. Done exclusively, or in isolation from the context of the entire play, monologue work can be indulgent, self-serving, and damaging. However, by exploring the entire character, the world of the play, the immediacy of the given circumstances, one can isolate a moment and genuinely gain from truthfully presenting such a moment (to a class, to a director, to a producer). The important element to this sort of *exercise* is the depth and fullness in which the actor works.

This volume of monologues offers cuttings of speeches from plays along with brief introductions that put the speeches in context. The brief introduction will help you select and focus your interest, but only in as much as it leads you to the full play and the rigors of creating a character in the same way you would work to play the entire role. It takes just as much to create a truthful moment as it does to create several truthful moments. Such work cannot be abridged and it would be wrong to interpret the intentions of this book to be a shortcut to quick-fix character creation. As teachers and directors we can always tell when an actor's character work has begun and ended with the printed text of the speech chosen for the solo presentation. In such situations, the work frequently appears flashy yet shallow, whereas the monologue that has been informed by the whole life of the character within the context of the entire play is vibrant and compelling.

As actors, we never stop studying. We urge you to explore this volume by finding speeches most suited to your interest and ability when presenting yourself in an audition situation, but, conversely, exploring bold and unusual speeches to work on when you are in class or working on your own to stretch your scope and technique. Like the musician, the actor needs constant attention to techniques. When the orchestra isn't in session, the musician spends hours alone tirelessly practicing solo pieces of music. So, too, when not in a play, the actor must keep tuning up the techniques of character. The monologue is one of the exercises that fits the actor tool kit and can yield much when approached with vigor and with truth. We hope that the monologues herein contribute to your depth of character work and serve you in your quest for excellence.

Craig Slaight and Jack Sharrar
San Francisco, 1998

Monologues
for
Young Women

. . .

Angels in America

by Tony Kushner

The Play: Subtitled a "Gay Fantasia on National Themes" and divided in two parts, "Millennium Approaches" and "Perostroika", Kushner's epic work probes politics, religion, sex, and human relationships in a manner that resonates throughout the universe.

Time and Place: From Washington, D.C., the South Bronx, Salt Lake City, Antarctica, and the Kremlin, to Hell, Heaven, Purgatory, and beyond. 1985–1990.

The Scene: Harper Pitt, an agoraphobic young Mormon woman with a Valium addiction, sits alone talking to herself. She is the wife of Joe Pitt, a young chief clerk for the Justice Department, who is struggling with his sexual identity.

• • •

(Harper at home, alone. She is listening to the radio and talking to herself as she often does. She speaks to the audience.)

HARPER: People who are lonely, people left alone, sit talking nonsense to the air, imagining...beautiful systems dying, old fixed orders spiraling apart... When you look at the ozone layer, from outside, from a spaceship, it looks like a pale blue halo, a gentle, shimmering aureole encircling the atmosphere encircling the earth. Thirty miles above our heads, a thin layer of three-atom oxygen molecules, product of photosynthesis, which explains the fussy vegetable preference for visible light, its rejection of darker rays and emanations. Danger from without. It's a kind of gift, from God, the crowning touch to the creation of the world: Guardian angels, hands linked, make a spherical net, a blue-green nesting orb, a shell of safety for life itself. But everywhere, things are collapsing, lies surfacing, systems of defense giving way... This is why, Joe, this is why I shouldn't be left alone. *(Little pause.)* I'd like to go traveling. Leave you behind to worry. I'll send postcards with strange stamps and tantalizing messages on the back. "Later maybe." "Nevermore..."

The Scene: *In the second speech from part two of the play, Harper is on a plane headed for San Francisco.*

• • •

(Night. Harper appears. She is in a window seat on board a jumbo jet, airborne.)

HARPER: Night flight to San Francisco. Chase the moon across America. God! It's been years since I was on a plane! When we hit thirty-five thousand feet, we'll have reached the tropopause. The great belt of calm air. As close as I'll ever get to the ozone. I dreamed we were there. The plane leapt the tropopause, the safe air, and attained the outer rim, the ozone, which was ragged and torn, patches of it threadbare as old cheesecloth, and that was frightening... But I saw something only I could see, because of my astonishing ability to see such things: Souls were rising, from the earth far below, souls of the dead, of people who had perished, from famine, from war, from the plague, and they floated up, like skydivers in reverse, limbs all akimbo, wheeling and spinning. And the souls of these departed joined hands, clasped ankles, and formed a web, a great net of souls, and the souls were three-atom oxygen molecules, of the stuff of ozone, and the outer rim absorbed them, and was repaired. Nothing's lost forever. In this world, there is a kind of painful progress. Longing for what we've left behind, and dreaming ahead. At least I think that's so.

Arcadia
by Tom Stoppard

The Play: Moving back and forth between the nineteenth and twentieth centuries, Arcadia examines the nature of truth and time and the contrast between Classical and Romantic sensibilities, among other issues.

Time and Place: A room on the garden front of a large country estate in Derbyshire, England. April, 1809.

The Scene: In the speech below, the young Thomasina is taking a lesson on Cleopatra and the classics from her handsome tutor, Septimus. See Septimus' speech in the section for men.

• • •

THOMASINA: Everything is turned to love with her. New love, absent love, lost love—I never knew a heroine that makes such noodles of our sex. It only needs a Roman general to drop anchor outside the window and away goes the empire like a christening mug into a pawn shop. If Queen Elizabeth had been a Ptolemy, history would have been quite different—we would be admiring the pyramids of Rome and the great Sphinx of Verona.

[SEPTIMUS: God save us.]

THOMASINA: But instead, the Egyptian noodle made carnal embrace with the enemy who burned the great library of Alexandria without so much as a fine for all that is overdue. Oh, Septimus!—can you bear it? All the lost plays of the Athenians! Two hundred at least by Aeschylus, Sophocles, Euripides—thousands of poems—Aristotle's own library brought to Egypt by the noodle's ancestors! How can we sleep for grief?

Aunt Dan and Lemon

by Wallace Shawn

The Play: Through a series of flashbacks, *Aunt Dan and Lemon* tells the chilling story of Lenora (Lemon), an intelligent somewhat fragile young English woman who falls under the spell of an older family friend, Danielle (Aunt Dan). Gradually Aunt Dan becomes the central force in Lemon's life, shaping and corrupting her moral view of what it means to be a human being. In the end, which is where the play begins, Lemon has come to believe that only brute force, such as the Nazis exhibited, is the true order for mankind.

Time and Place: The present in the London flat of Lenora.

The Scene: Lenora (Lemon) speaks of her philosophy of life and how she acquired it.

• • •

(The dark room, as at the beginning of the play.)

LEMON: *(To the audience.)* There's something that people never say about the Nazis now. *(She drinks.)* By the way, how can anybody like anything better than lime and celery juice? It is the best! The thing is that the Nazis were trying to create a certain way of life for themselves. That's obvious if you read these books I'm reading. They believed that the primitive society of the Germanic tribes had created a life of wholeness and meaning for each person. They blamed the sickness and degeneracy of society as *they* knew it—before they came to power, of course—on the mixture of races that had taken place since that tribal period. In their opinion, all the destructive values of greed, materialism, competitiveness, dishonesty, and so on, had been brought into their society by non-Germanic races. They may have been wrong about it, but that was their belief. So they were trying to create a certain way of life. They were trying to create, or re-create, some sort of society of brothers, bound together by a certain code of loyalty and honor. So to make that attempt, they had to remove the non-Germans, they had to eliminate inter-breeding. They were trying to create a certain way of life. Now today, of course, everybody says, "How awful! How awful!" And they were certainly ruthless and thorough in what they did. But the mere fact of killing human beings in order to create a certain way of life is not something that exactly distinguishes the Nazis from everybody else. That's just absurd. When any people feels that its hopes for a desirable future are threatened by some other group, they always do the very same thing. The only question is the degree of the threat. Now for us, for example, criminals are a threat, but they're only a small threat. Right now, we would say about criminals that they're a serious annoyance. We would call them a problem. And right now, the way we deal with that problem is that we take the criminals and we put them in jail. But if these criminals became so vicious, if there got to be so many of them, that our most basic hopes as a society were truly threatened by them—if our whole system of prisons and policemen had fallen so far behind the problem that the streets of our cities were controlled and dominated by violent criminals—then we would find ourselves forgetting the prisons and just killing the criminals instead. It's just a fact. Or let's take the Communists. There are Communists, now, who meet in little groups in America and England. They don't disrupt our entire way of life. They just have their meetings. If they break a law, if they commit a crime, we punish them according to the penalty prescribed. But in some countries, they threaten to destroy their whole way of life. In those countries the Communists are strong, they're violent, they're actually fanatics. And usually it turns out that people decide that they have to be killed. Or when the Europeans first came to America, well, the Indians were there. The Indians fought them for every scrap of land. There was no chance to build the kind of society the Europeans wanted with the Indians there. If they'd tried to put all the Indians in jail, they would have had to put all their effort into building jails, and then, when the Indians came out, they would undoubtedly have started fighting all over again as hard as before. And so they decided to kill the Indians. So it becomes absurd to talk about the Nazis as if the Nazis were unique. That's a kind of hypocrisy. Because the fact is, no society has ever considered the taking of life an unpardonable crime or even, really, a major tragedy. It's something that's done when it has to be done, and it's as simple as that. It's no different from the fact that if I have harmful or obnoxious insects—let's say, cockroaches—living in my house, I probably have to do something about it. Or at least, the question I have to ask is: How many are there? If the cockroaches are small, and I see a few of them now and then, that may not be very disturbing to me. But if I see big ones, if I start to see them often, then I say to myself, they have to be killed. Now some people simply hate to kill cockroaches, so they'll wait much longer. But if the time comes when there are hundreds of them, when they're crawling out of every drawer, when they're in the oven, when they're in the refrigerator, when they're in the toilet, when they're in the bed, then even the person who hates to kill them will go to the shop and get some poison and start killing, because the way of life that that person had wanted to lead is now really being threatened. Yes, the fact is, it is very unpleasant to kill another creature—let's admit it. Each one of us has his own fear of pain and his own fear of death. It's true for people and for every type of creature that lives. I remember once squashing a huge brown roach—I slammed it with my shoe, but it wasn't dead and I sat and watched it, and it's an awful period just before any creature dies—any insect or animal—when you're watching the stupid, ignorant things that that creature is trying to do to fight off its death— whether it's moving its arms or its legs, or it's kicking, or it's trying to crawl to another part of the floor, or it's trying to lift itself off the ground—those things can't prevent death!—but the creature is trying out every gesture it's capable of, hoping, hoping that something will help it. And I remember how I felt as I watched that big brown roach squirming and crawling, and yet it was totally squashed, and I could see its insides slowly come oozing out. And I'm sure that the bigger a thing is, the more you hate to see it. I remember when I was in school we did some experiments on these big rats, and we had to inject them with poison and watch them die—and, of course, no matter what humane method you use in any laboratory to kill the animals, there's a moment that comes when they sense what's happening and they start to try out all these telltale squirming gestures. And with people, of course, it's the same thing. The bigger the creature, the harder it is to kill. We know it takes at least ten minutes to hang a person. Even if you shoot them in the head, it's not instantaneous—they still make those squirming movements at least for a moment. And people in gas chambers rush to the doors that they know very well are firmly locked. They fight each other to get to the doors. So killing is always very unpleasant. Now when people say, "Oh the Nazis were different from anyone, the Nazis were different from anyone," well, perhaps that's true in at least one way, which is that they observed themselves extremely frankly in the act of killing, and they admitted frankly how they really felt about the whole process. Yes, of course, they admitted, it's very unpleasant, and if we didn't have to do it in order to create a way of life that we want for ourselves, we would never be involved in killing at all. But since we have to do it, why not be truthful about it, and why not admit that yes, yes, there's something inside us that likes to kill. Some part of us. There's something inside us that likes to do it. Why shouldn't that be so? Our human nature is derived from the nature of different animals, and of course there's a part of animal nature that likes to kill. If killing were totally repugnant to animals, they couldn't survive. So an enjoyment of killing is somewhere inside us, somewhere in our nature. In polite society, people don't discuss it, but the fact is that it's enjoyable—it's enjoyable—to make plans for killing, and it's enjoyable to learn about killing that is done by other people, and it's enjoyable to think about killing, and it's enjoyable to read about killing, and it's even enjoyable actually to kill, although when we ourselves are actually killing, an element of unpleasantness always comes in. That unpleasant feeling starts to come in. But even there, one has to say, even though there's an unpleasant side at first to watching people die, we have to admit that after watching for a while—maybe after watching for a day or maybe for a week or a year—it's still in a way unpleasant to watch, but on the other hand we have to admit that after we've watched it for all that time—well, we don't really actually care any more. We have to admit that we don't really care. And I think that that last admission is what really makes people go mad about the Nazis, because in our own society we have this kind of cult built up around what people call the feeling of "compassion." I remember my mother screaming all the time, "Compassion! Compassion! You have to have compassion for other people! You have to have compassion for other human beings!" And I must admit, there's something I find refreshing about the Nazis, which is partly why I enjoy reading about them every night, because they sort of had the nerve to say, "Well, what *is* this compassion? Because I don't really know what it is. So I want to know, really, what is it?" And they must have sort of asked each other at some point, "Well say, Heinz, have *you* ever felt it?" "Well no, Rolf, what about you?" And they all had to admit that they really didn't know what the hell it was. And I find it sort of relaxing to read about those people, because I have to admit that I don't know either. I mean, I think I've felt it reading a novel, and I think I've felt it watching a film—"Oh how sad, that child is sick! That mother is crying!"—but I can't ever remember feeling it in life. I just don't remember feeling it about something that was happening in front of my eyes. And I can't believe that other people are that different from me. In other words, it was unpleasant to watch that pitiful roach scuttling around on my floor dying, but I can't say I really felt *sad* about it. I felt revolted or sickened, I guess I would say, but I can't say that I really felt sorry for the roach. And plenty of people have cried in my presence or seemed to be suffering, and I remember wishing they'd *stop* suffering and *stop* crying and leave me alone, but I don't remember, frankly, that I actually cared. So you have to say finally, well, fine, if there are all these people like my mother who want to go around talking about compassion all day, well, fine, that's their right. But it's sort of refreshing to admit every once in a while that they're talking about something that possibly doesn't exist. And it's sort of an ambition of mine to go around some day and ask each person I meet, Well here is something you've heard about to the point of nausea all of your life, but do you personally, actually remember feeling it, and if you really do, could you please describe the particular circumstances in which you felt it and what it actually felt *like?* Because if there's one thing I learned from Aunt Dan, I suppose you could say it was a kind of honesty. It's easy to say we should all be loving and sweet, but meanwhile we're enjoying a certain way of life—and we're actually *living*—due to the existence of certain other people who are willing to take the job of killing on their own backs, and it's not a bad thing every once in a while to admit that that's the way we're living, and even to give to those certain people a tiny, fractional crumb of thanks. You can be very sure that it's more than they expect, but I think they'd be grateful, all the same.

(The lights fade as she sits and drinks.)

The Ballad of Yachiyo
by Philip Kan Gotanda

The Play: Yachiyo, a poor peasant girl with not much hope of raising herself beyond working in the sugar fields of Hawaii, is sent by her father to live with a pottery artist, Hiro Takamura, and his wife, Okusan. Okusan hopes to teach Yachiyo proper Japanese language and customs, and before long Hiro finds new inspiration for his work through the girl. Eventually the young Yachiyo and Hiro develop a deep relationship that leads to a tragic outcome.

Time and Place: Kauai, Hawaiian Islands, 1919.

The Scene: The following two monologues bookend the play. In the first, Yachiyo paints a picture of Takamura practicing his art.

• • •

YACHIYO: In front of him sits a mound of clay which he is squeezing into a tall cone, he pushes it down, then squeezes it into a tall cone again. This helps to even the consistency of the clay and makes it easier to work with. All during this he is pulling on the base of the wheel with his feet to keep it turning.

    [TAKAMURA: *(Calling out.)* I need more clay, prepare more clay for me!]

YACHIYO: He is making *yunomi,* teacups. Takamura-san does this by working the clay back into a tall cone and by fashioning a measured portion at the top into a ball. He's done this so many times he knows just the amount to use by the feel. Then by inserting the thumb of his right hand he makes a deep pocket, drawing the clay up to make the walls of the cup with the same thumb and middle finger. It's all done in one motion. Now he starts to use some tools. First, he inserts a flat spatulate tool to make sure the *yunomi* has a clean surface on the inside. Then, he takes a *tombo,* dragonfly, because of the way it looks—

[TAKAMURA: *(Looking up, interrupting gruffly.)* Yachiyo, *hayaku shiro!* Hurry up! *(Takamura fades to black. Silence.)*]

YACHIYO: Just before the sun breaks it gets very dark. Inky black and silent. As if all the light and sound has been sucked out of the air. The wind dies, night birds stop singing and everything seems to be suspended. Waiting. This is my favorite time of day. It's so dark that the boundary between the night and my body blurs and I begin to come undone, as if I am a child again, my Mama's hands unbuttoning me, my Papa putting me to sleep. And I can drift, let go, releasing out into this night my sweat, my breath. my thirst. My shame...

[(The sun begins to slowly rise. Upstage in half light we see the silhouettes of Papa and Mama stirring from sleep.)

PAPA: Yachiyo? Yachiyo?

MAMA: What is it Papa?

PAPA: Yachiyo, is that you? Yachiyo?

(Morning light begins to break the horizon. Yachiyo turns away from Papa and Mama as they fade to black.)]

YACHIYO: It is a beautiful morning. The night was filled with many dreams and when I woke up, I was happy. I cannot remember any of them, the dreams, and yet I have this silly smile on my face. *(Picking up a worn leather suitcase and moving across the stage.)* I was born on the island of Kauai. On the leeward side just beyond Camp Mana in an area called Saki-Mana. It's the dry side of the island. The soil is reddish in color and when you walk barefoot in it you leave a trail of red prints wherever you go. *(Glancing back at her path.)* Papa says you don't need to know where you came from. Mama says you do. *(Pause.)* The year is 1919. I am sixteen years old. My name is Yachiyo Matsumoto...

The Scene: In this second monologue, Yachiyo enters the waters of Polihale Beach.

• • •

YACHIYO: Polihale Beach. The water. It's like a mirror... I enter and swim out far beyond the breaking waves. My arms ache and my legs already weary from walking all night begin to cramp. But I continue to push out until the shore appears a distant shadow. *(Noticing.)* The sun...rising like a swarm of dark insects... *(She watches the sun breaking the horizon.)* And then I dive. Deep beneath the surface. I must see the world from the other side. Through her eyes.

(Lights and sound.)

YACHIYO: My face feeling the cold lick of salt and wetness. Deeper and deeper, straining my arms, kicking with my legs. Forcing myself to go farther and farther down. The boundary between the night and my body blurring, blackness everywhere, my air running out. My shame... I must push myself down, down—I must go so far. So far that I cannot come back... He loved her very deeply, he loved her very deeply...

(Pause. Sound cue builds as Yachiyo realizes she has no air left. She panics, changes her mind. Overhead a light appears representing the surface above.)

YACHIYO: No air, no air left, I'm choking, suffocating—I have to get back to the surface, I need to breathe, I need to breathe so badly I can feel my face about to explode. I see the sunlight entering from above. Cutting through the water like long transparent knives. I want them to cut me open, peel me out of my skin so whatever is me, whatever is wanting, needing to breathe so badly can get out...

(She struggles fiercely. Blackout. Deep, echoey, crash. Mama and Papa, sleeping in half light, begin to stir.)

[PAPA: *(Waking up.)* Yachiyo? Yachiyo?
MAMA: What is it Papa?
PAPA: Yachiyo, is that you? Yachiyo…
(Yachiyo is lit. Light goes from warm to brighter and brighter during the following speech.)]
YACHIYO: The wind dies, night birds stop singing and everything seems to be suspended. Waiting. And I can drift, let go, releasing out into this night my sweat, my breath, my thirst, my…

Balm in Gilead
by Lanford Wilson

The Play: *Balm in Gilead* is a kaleidoscopic slice of life that centers on two characters Joe and Darlene, who have some hope of escaping the ugly world they have fallen into among the drug addicts, pimps, and petty criminals of New York's upper Broadway.

Time and Place: The late sixties; the entire action is set in an all-night coffee shop on New York's upper Broadway.

The Scene: Darlene is talking to Ann about "boyfriend" stuff and life in general.

• • •

DARLENE: *(Laughs.)* I know what you mean. That's funny. *(Pause.)* Those two that always sit around in here, you know; the dark headed one and she's got a little baby? Are they married? Or do you know?

[ANN: I don't know. No one knows. I don't imagine, but they'd probably tell you they were.]

DARLENE: It's a cute little baby, really. I don't know if I'd bring him here at all hours of the day and night like that if it was mine, though.

[ANN: Well, some people would give anything to look respectable.]

DARLENE: *(Pause.)* I know one thing: I sure feel like you do about marriage. I mean, I just don't know. Like you said. I know this guy I used to go with—when I first got a room of my own, up on Armitage Street? Do you know that part of Chicago?

[ANN: No. But then I was only four.]

DARLENE: Oh. Well, most of the streets run either east and west or up and down, you know—one or the other. But some of them kinna cut across all the others—Armitage Street does, and some of the other real nice ones. Fullerton Street does.

(I don't know if it's important, but Fullerton Street does not. In other words, Darlene rather prefers the vivid to the accurate.)

DARLENE: And they're wider, you know, with big trees and all, and there are all of these big old lovely apartment buildings, very well taken care of, with little lawns out front and flower boxes in the windows and all. You know what I mean? And the rents, compared to what they try to sock you with here. The rents are practically nothing—even in this neighborhood. *(Pause.)* My apartment was two flights up, in the front. It was so cute, you'd have loved it. They had it all done over when I moved in. I had three rooms. And let's see—there was just a lovely big living room that looked out onto Armitage Street and a real cute little kitchen and then the bedroom—that looked out onto a garden in the back and on the other side of the garden was Grant Park—or some park, I never did know the name it had. But there were kids that I just loved playing out in this park all the time. And then I had this little bathroom, a private bath. I had—it was funny—I had a collection—you know practically everybody collects something…

[ANN: Yeah, I know what you mean.]

DARLENE: *(Laughs.)* I collected towels, if you must know. You know, from all the big hotels—of course, I didn't get very many of them myself, but friends of mine, every time they went anywhere always brought me back a big bath towel or hand towel or face towel with some new name across it. I'll swear, I never bought one towel in all the time I lived there! It was funny, too, it looked real great in a regular bathroom like that; these hotel names. Everyone just loved it. My favorite one was—from this—oh, this real elegant hotel— what was it's—I don't even remember the name anymore I had so many of them. Anyway, the apartment, in that neighborhood and all, cost me practically nothing compared to what they want for a place not half as good in New York. And

I lived there, and this guy I was going with, you know, that asked me to marry him? He lived across the hall. He moved into the apartment next to mine. Really, Ann, you should have seen him. He was slow, everything he did, and quiet; he hardly ever talked at all. You had to just pump him to get him to say the time of day. And he had white hair—nearly white; they used to call him Cotton—he told me—when he was in Alabama. That's where he's from. He was living in the apartment next to mine and we were always together, and there just wasn't any difference between his place and mine. We should have only been paying for one rent. Half of his stuff was in my place and half vice versa. He used to get so pissed off when I'd wash things out and hang them up in his bathroom or in the kitchen and all. You know, over the fire there. But we were always together—and we finally decided to get married—we both did. And all our friends were buying rice and digging out their old shoes. Cotton—he worked in a television factory, RCA, I believe, but I couldn't be sure. That's why I started thinking about him when you said this Sam had electrical parts all over the apartment. Old Cotton had, I'll swear, the funniest temperament I ever saw. If he got mad— (Almost as though mad.)—he wouldn't argue or anything like that, he'd just walk around like nothing was wrong only never say one word. Sometimes for two or three days. And that used to get me so mad I couldn't stand it. Have you ever known anyone who did that?

[ANN: Yeah, I know what you mean.]

DARLENE: Just wouldn't talk at all, I mean. Not say one word for days.

[ANN: It sounds familiar enough.]

DARLENE: It used to just burn me up. And he knew it did, is what made it so bad. I'd just be so mad I could spit. And I'd say something like; what's wrong, Cotton? And just as easy as you please he'd reach over and light a cigarette and look out the window or something. Turn on the radio. I just wish I had the control to be like that because it is the most maddening thing you can possibly to do someone when they're trying to argue with you. I could do it for about five minutes, then I'd blow my stack. Oh, I used to get so damn mad at him. Agh! *(Pause.)* Course I make it sound worse than it was, cause he didn't act like that very often. Fortunately. But you never knew what was going to provoke him, I swear. It was just that we saw each other every hour of every day—you just couldn't get us apart. And when we decided to get married all our friends were so excited—of course, they'd been expecting it probably. But we were so crazy you'd never know what we were going to do. I know he used to set the TV so it pointed into the mirror, because there wasn't a plug-in by the bed and we'd lay there in bed and look at the mirror that had the TV reflected in it. Only everything was backwards. Writing was backwards. *(She laughs.)* Only, you know, even backwards, it was a better picture, it was clearer than if you was just looking straight at it.

A Bird of Prey

by Jim Grimsley

The Play: A modern tragedy set in a large city in California where the young people face good and evil on their own terms, with calamitous consequences. When Monty's dysfunctional family moves to a complex urban environment from rural Louisiana, Monty attempts to find genuine faith, while at the same time struggling to shield his younger siblings from the temptation and danger they encounter everywhere.

Time and Place: The 1990s. An Unnamed City.

The Scene: A local boy, Corvette, has been missing for a few days. No one knows where he is or what happened, although speculation amongst his contemporaries is wild, especially from Donna, who is a close friend of Corvette and who feels she knows more than the others. In the first speech, Donna shares her innermost fears.

• • •

DONNA: It's me now. I'm the one. I have to hurry because Hilda and Tracey are coming soon, but I'm here. I guess I'm praying you know? I don't guess anybody's there but I'm talking to somebody. We need help. *(Pause.)* You know who I mean. All of us. *(Pause.)* I feel like I really am talking to somebody, like somebody really is there. You know? Do you get that feeling sometimes? That you're speaking in a room where you're absolutely alone except there is somebody with you, invisible. Who hears everything you say. I wish that were true. *(Pause.)* I know things nobody else knows. *(Pause.)* I kept watching Corvette those last few days. I talked to him. I know he's dead now, I know he didn't just run away, and I keep thinking about that last conversation. I talked to him and he seemed like he was burning up with something. He had met somebody.

He talked about this man. Just for a minute. This older guy. And when he did his eyes, they were like, I don't know. Like prey. Like he was watching something swoop down on him, and he wanted it. He wasn't scared, but he was hooked on something, not a drug but something else, a feeling. He wouldn't say much, and then he tried to act normal again, and when I asked him a question about this man he just laughed. But I was so scared, because of the look in his eyes. Like he would be killed in the next second and he wanted it. And right then I wondered what his life had been like, to make him feel like that. He had lived on my street forever, he was my neighbor since he was a kid, and all of a sudden I felt like I hardly knew him. And he went away with Thacker and I never saw him again. But when I heard he had disappeared, I knew. *(Pause.)* I never told anybody I talked to him. When I close my eyes I can still see the look on his face. *(Pause.)* It's the way Monty looks, sometimes. Like there's somebody waiting for him, too. *(Pause.)* I know he talks to somebody, when he's alone, I know he's not embarrassed to call it praying, like I am. But he needs it. Somebody's got to help him, if he's going to escape. Somebody.

The Scene: *Monty's young sister, Marie (thirteen), struggles with the torment of a fractured and abusive family life. In a moment alone, on her way home from school, Marie confesses her need for the protection and fullness of school life.*

• • •

MARIE: I'm going home, I'm walking behind Monty and Evan, and I'm being quiet so Evan won't punch me in the shoulder, I'm going home like I'm supposed to, but I don't want to go. All day in school it's been peaceful, with nobody bothering me, except Marie in my math class who hates that we have the same name. Except for her they leave me alone, and I like that. All day I sit there with my books and do what I'm supposed to do. Everything is calm all day. But school doesn't last long enough, I have to go home at the end of every day, and when the bell rings I get all hollow inside, and I pack up my books and go outside to wait for Monty and Evan. We walk home the long way, we go pretty slow, and we never talk, unless we're arguing about something. We're all thinking the same thing, we're all wondering what it will be like when we get home, and I hate that feeling, I hate not knowing. I wish it would be peaceful, I think about it the whole way home, and sometimes it is. Sometimes Mama comes to walk us home instead of Monty, and I can tell by the way she looks whether it's okay at home or not. If she's smiling and she's brushed her hair and if she looks me in the eye, then everything's all right. But if she's standing there with her arms all wrapped around herself and her hair pulled back and she's looking at the ground, I know it's not okay, I know they're fighting again. I don't want to go home then, more than anything. But I don't have any choice. I wish school lasted longer. Sometimes I wish it lasted so long I would have to spend the night. I told that to my friend Candy, we have most of our classes together, and she likes me; I told her I wish I could stay in school all the time, but she didn't understand. She says I need a boyfriend, that's all I need, but I think about my dad and I don't know if I want one or not.

Class Action
by Brad Slaight

The Play: A collage of encounters and solos occurring outside the classroom, reveals the difficulties of coming-of-age in the complex environment of high school.

Time and Place: A year in the 1990s. Various parts of an unnamed high school.

The Scene: Emma (teen) recounts a life-altering encounter at a famous rock concert.

• • •

EMMA: I screamed when the DJ told me I had not only won tickets to the concert, but backstage passes as well. *(She displays a backstage pass.)* I mean I had never won anything in my life, and then all of a sudden I was caller number twenty-five and on my way to the biggest concert of the year! The New Landlords were my favorite group, and the fact that I was going to get to meet them kept me from getting much sleep the rest of the week. The concert was everything I hoped it would be, I had the best seat in the house and my friend Cindy owed me big time for giving her the other ticket. She just about passed out when we went backstage to meet the band members. Eddie was my favorite and I almost fainted when they introduced him to me. He was the lead singer, and not really that much older than me, even though he looked like he was. Cindy was so caught up with all the excitement, she didn't see Eddie and me leave the party and go to his dressing room. *(Pause.)* I guess I should have known what was going on, but I honestly thought we were just going to get away from the noise and have a good talk. Eddie and me alone together, it was like a dream or something! His lyrics are so inspiring, so full of love that I was completely shocked when he pulled me over to a couch and started tearing at my clothes. Maybe if he would have kissed me or something first I wouldn't have reacted like I did, but he moved on me so quick. He got on top of me and started pulling at my shirt. He was much stronger than me and even though I pushed and told him no, he pinned me down. I started to panic because I felt trapped and he wouldn't listen to me. His rough beard was scratching my face. His breath made me nauseous. When he started to unzip his pants it gave me just enough room to swing my knee hard into his crotch, causing him to fall off me. I got out of there before he could go any further. *(Pause.)* I saw him on MTV the next week. He had makeup on, but I could still see the scratch marks where I gouged his face. I hope it never heals. *(She looks at the backstage pass and tosses it on the ground as she exits.)*

The Scene: *Danielle (teen) reveals a secret that will soon be very public.*

• • •

DANIELLE: I haven't started to show yet, so most everyone thinks that I'm moody because I broke up with Richie. That's partly true, although I don't blame him for not wanting the burden of having this kid. We're both only seventeen. He wanted me to "take care of it," and even though I believe in the whole choice thing, my choice was to keep her. Oh, I know it will be a "girl" because I'm hardly sick or anything, and my Aunt Susan told me that it's always baby boys that make a pregnant woman nauseous. She should know…she had four. My Aunt Susan's been real cool about this. I told her before I told anybody, because we've always had a special friendship. Richie doesn't talk to me much anymore, and I'm sure some of my friends are going to be pretty weird around me when I start swelling. But somehow none of that seems to matter. I know that I'll be able to handle all the problems that come along because there is someone who is much more important than all of them put together. And she is inside me now. Waiting to help me. Waiting to need me.

Cleveland

by Mac Wellman

The Play: "A poem (or in this case a play) should not mean but be", to borrow from John Ciardi.

Time and Place: Cleveland during prom season and in the dreamtime of seventeen-year-old Joan. The present.

The Scene: The prom. In the Men's Room. The Mayor of Cleveland, who has been serving as a chaperone, has his head stuck in a towel dispenser. As others look for just the right tool to unwedge the Mayor, Joan holds vigil. Note: Some of the vocabulary is Mirandan whispertalk. This alien language only consists of consonants, except for an occasional ending. Mainly sibilants and fricatives. Vowels are open. C is pronounced like ch *in* church.

• • •

JOAN: Don't worry Mister Mayor. I'll stand watch over you. You had a kind word for my father even though he was a Trotskyite and you being a fashionable Mayor and Public Figure and all in all quite the thing. Everyday despair gets to a person when they're trapped by the limits of their ecosystems... Back home in Skyeyesqll the air's so thick you could stir it with a spoon. My real father's an Xylmn. They don't have Xylmns here, and I guess it would take too long to explain what that is and you've got problems of your own. Enemies of our Way have tried to force the issue. Inglefinger, my fake mother, got more than she bargained for. We're a tough people. We never look back and when we do a thing we do it right. Still, Triton's not much to look at. Old Queen Larav needs the spinal fluid for her wind machines. Out that far if you don't keep the air in motion it freezes up. And that's a sticky situation. I can tell you. I know. Isn't this corsage nice? Richard's a nice boy. Panda Hands. Not a bad dancer. There are more of them around here. Mirandans, I mean. I'll be one of the missing. Others will take my place. Uranus, our sister planet, has a pretty, velvet ring, black as coal. It glitters in the night sky like black pearls. I sing and dance a lot. On my days off. Would you believe I'm nearly five-hundred thousand years old. A Pisces. Mr. Mayor, I like Cleveland and well I'll miss school. Our Lady of the Bleeding Knuckle. Our Lady of the Runny Nose. There aren't any Catholics on Triton. No Trotskyites either. We have a different way of doing things. We keep whatever daylight reaches us in these little stone jars. Sometimes the whole Plain of Qqqsmsmccctu is covered with them. Our enemies on Miranda are pretty dumb. We've almost got them beat. Another few centuries at most they say. I'll miss my girlfriends, especially Losin' Susan. She's a riot. I think she's still a virgin. Who knows? But Inglefinger's right. Miranda's a prettier place than Triton. That's why we want it. Our rhinodraconopeds need it for grazing. Tough shit, you Mirandans! I figured out my Pope Joan dream. It was about how worried I was about the prom and feeling bad because I got stuck with old Panda Hands. You want to hear some Whispertalk? "Skrxxsx. Kxrs. Bkssxx. Xs. Bkxxxllxxxllmnnmcc…" That's the first line of a poem about the Sea of Kxrs. Frozen methane. Looks a little like Lake Erie. Panda Hands will want to go and make out behind the shopping center. But I'm gonna tell him I want to go to Indiana. Will he ever be excited! A pllptptcccplpu's there waiting to take me home. You ever seen a time feather? This *(Holds it up.)* is one. Pretty isn't it? I'll tell you a secret. I don't love Jimmy the Door anymore. Want to hear one of our songs? *(She sings a strange song.)* In the land of Tlpccc the trees grow upside down, but nobody knows they do. *(Pause.)* Tlpccc, that's like China. On the other side of the world. Get it? *(She whistles a refrain.)*

The Conduct of Life
by Maria Irene Fornes

The Play: In a series of nineteen scenes, *The Conduct of Life* depicts the emotional torture and psychological and physical brutality exacted on several women by the men in their lives. There is much wisdom and insight into the human condition and the suffering some women have endured throughout history.

Time and Place: A Latin American Country. The present.

The Scene: Twelve-year-old Nena, recalls her destitute life in a home for girls.

• • •

NENA: I used to clean beans when I was in the home. And also string beans. I also pressed clothes. The days were long. Some girls did hand sewing. They spent the day doing that. I didn't like it. When I did that, the day was even longer and there were times when I couldn't move even if I tried. And they said I couldn't go there anymore that I had to stay in the yard. I didn't mind sitting in the yard looking at the birds. I went to the laundry room and watched the women work. They let me go in and sit there. And they showed me how to press. I like to press because my mind wanders and I find satisfaction. I can iron all day. I like the way the wrinkles come out and things look nice. It's a miracle isn't it? I could earn a living pressing clothes. And I could find my grandpa and take care of him.

[OLIMPIA: Where is your grandpa?]

NENA: He sleeps in the streets. Because he's too old to remember where he lives. He needs a person to take care of him. And I can take care of him. But I don't know where he is—he doesn't know where I am—he doesn't know who he is. He's too old. He doesn't know anything about himself. He only knows how to beg. And he knows that, only because he's hungry. He walks around and begs for food. He forgets to go home. He lives in the camp for the homeless and he has his own box. It's not an ugly box like the others. It is a real box. I used to live there with him. He took me with him when my mother died till they took me to the home. It is a big box. It's big enough for two. I could sleep in the front where it's cold. And he could sleep in the back where it's warmer. And he could lean on me. The floor is hard for him because he's skinny and it's hard on his poor bones. He could sleep on top of me if that would make him feel comfortable. I wouldn't mind. Except that he may pee on me because he pees in his pants. He doesn't know not to. He is incontinent. He can't hold it. His box was a little smelly. But that doesn't matter because I could clean it. All I would need is some soap. I could get plenty of water from the public faucet. And I could borrow a brush. You know how clean I could get it? As clean as new. You know what I would do? I would make holes in the floor so the pee would go down to the ground. And you know what else I would do?

The Scene: *When Leticia, the mistress of the household, asks the servant girl, Olimpia, to help her with a task the inflexible Olimpia details her daily routine.*

• • •

OLIMPIA: *(In a mumble.)* As soon as I finish doing this. You can't just ask me to do what you want me to do, and interrupt what I'm doing. I don't stop from the time I wake up in the morning to the time I go to sleep. You can't interrupt me whenever you want, not if you want me to get to the end of my work. I wake up at 5:30. I wash. I put on my clothes and make my bed. I go to the kitchen. I get the milk and the bread from outside and I put them on the counter. I open the icebox. I put one bottle in and take the butter out. I leave the other bottle on the counter. I shut the refrigerator door. I take the pan that I use for water and put water in it. I know how much. I put the pan on the stove, light the stove, cover it. I take the top off the milk and pour it in the milk pan except for a little. *(Indicating with her finger.)* Like this. For the cat. I put the pan on the stove, light the stove. I put coffee in the thing. I know how much. I light the oven and put bread in it. I come here, get the tablecloth and I lay it on the table. I shout "Breakfast." I get the napkins. I take the cups, the saucers, and the silver out and set the table. I go to the kitchen. I put the tray on the counter, put the butter on the tray. The water and the milk are getting hot. I pick up the cat's dish. I wash it. I pour the milk I left in the bottle in the milk dish. I put it on the floor for the cat. I shout "Breakfast." The water boils. I pour it in the thing. When the milk boils I turn off the gas and cover the milk. I get the bread from the oven. I slice it down the middle and butter it. Then I cut it in pieces *(Indicating.)* this big. I set a piece aside for me. I put the rest of the bread in the bread dish and shout "Breakfast." I pour the coffee in the coffeepot and the milk in the milk pitcher, except I leave *(Indicating.)* this much for me. I put them on the tray and bring them here. If you're not in the dining room I call again. "Breakfast." I go to the kitchen, I fill the milk pan with water and let it soak. I pour my coffee, sit at the counter and eat my breakfast. I go upstairs to make your bed and clean your bathroom. I come down here to meet you and figure out what you want for lunch and dinner. And try to get you to think quickly so I can run to the market and get it bought before all the fresh stuff is bought up. Then, I start the day.

Death Comes to Us All, Mary Agnes

by Christopher Durang

The Play: A bizarre, biting, darkly humorous look at the Pommes, a family on the periphery of life.

Time and Place: The Pomme's decaying mansion. The present.

The Scene: Margot conjures up a painful memory with Grandma, who has just suffered a bad episode herself.

• • •

MARGOT: *(Bringing Mrs. Jansen-Hubbell to sofa.)* Grandma, do you remember me? It's your little Margot. Sit down, let me look at you. Do you remember me? I remember you, way back before you first feigned madness. Do you remember that summer I was fifteen, and Daddy and I came to visit right after he'd found the French orphanage my mother had put me in? And Grandad had just got the first of his secretaries. Remember? It was Miss Willis, then, I think. And I asked you why Mama had put me in an orphanage like I didn't belong to her, just so she could go to Italy with her two boys, her two sons, my twin brothers! She left me there for five years! *(Getting teary and hysterical.)* And I said to you, Grandma, will there ever be anyone in the world who will love me? Love *me* for what I am, and love me and not pity me? And you looked at me and you said. "No," and I said, "But Grandma, Why?" And you said, "Because there never was for me!" Do you remember, Grandma? There never was for me!

The Scene: Margot tells her father about one of her disturbing dreams.

• • •

MARGOT: Last night I had that awful dream again.

[HERBERT: Margot, you work yourself up over nothing. Lots of girls dream they're Joan of Arc.]

MARGOT: *(Angry.)* I don't mean the Joan of Arc dream. This is the one where I'm in the orphanage and I see my mother in a field with my two brothers, canoeing. And rather than feeling angry at her for putting me in the orphanage, I just feel this terrible longing to be accepted by them, by her. And then I find that I'm dressed like a boy and that I've even grown a mustache, and I go out to them to show my mother that I'm a boy and then I notice that I'm still wearing lipstick, and I try to wipe it off but there's so much of it I can't get it off, and I keep wiping it and wiping it, and the three of them just laugh and laugh at me, and then they steer their canoe at me and it comes racing toward me to crush me, and a great big oar from the canoe hits me on top of the head, and then the oar starts to beat me repeatedly, ecstatically. And then I wake up. Trembling.

[HERBERT: What do you want me to say? The oar's a phallic symbol. You should stay away from boating. Don't grow a mustache.]

MARGOT: *(Takes his book, throws it across the room.)* I feel such anger and unhappiness all the time! When you rescued me from the orphanage, I thought I was finally saved and that things would be all right. But they weren't. You don't hate mother. And you don't like me. What am I to do? I've been seeing my psychiatrist for three years now, four times a week, and I don't feel any change. I feel such a prisoner to my past. And I have such a longing for normality. I see people on the street who eat in cafeterias and have families and go to parks and who aren't burdened with this terrible bitterness; and I want to be like them. So much I want to be like them.

Early Dark
by Reynolds Price

The Play: Rosacoke Mustian and members of her family struggle with life in northeastern North Carolina, attempting to seek love and purpose amidst complex internal and external turmoil.

Time and Place: Summer, fall and winter 1957. Warren County, North Carolina, and Mason's Lake, Virginia.

The Scene: In this first scene in the play, Rosacoke declares the depth of her love for Wesley, gone these two years, and expected at any moment to appear on the road just beyond the open window in which Rosacoke sits.

• • •

ROSACOKE: *(Still at the window, facing out; realizing as she goes.)* He's what I want... He's always been...[since] seven years this November. You had punished me for laughing that morning in church, and I wanted to die—which was nothing unusual—but guessed I could live if I breathed a little air, so I picked up a bucket and walked to the woods to hunt some nuts and win you back. It was getting on late. I was hoping you were worried. I was past Mr. Isaac's in the really deep woods. The leaves were all gone, but I hadn't found a nut. Still I knew of one tree Mildred Sutton had showed me—I was headed for that—and I found it finally. It was loaded—pecans the size of sparrows—and in the top fork a boy, a stranger to me. I was not even scared. He seemed to live there, twenty yards off the ground, staring out dead-level. I said "Are you strong enough to shake your tree?"—"If I wanted to," he said. I said "Well, want to please; I'm standing here hungry." He thought and then braced his long legs and arms and rocked four times—pecans nearly killed me. I rummaged round and filled my bucket, my pockets. He had still not faced me; so I said "Don't you want to share some of my pecans?" Then he looked down and smiled and said "I heard they were God's." I said "No, really they belong to Mr. Isaac Alston. He can't see this far."—"I can see him," he said. "You may can see Philadelphia," I said—he was looking back north—and he nodded to that but didn't look down. "How old are you?" I said. He said "Fifteen" and shut up again. "I'm thirteen," I said. He said "You'll live" and smiled once more toward Philadelphia and I came on home. I wanted him then and every day since.

The Fantasticks

By Tom Jones and Harvey Schmidt

The Play: This, the longest running off-Broadway musical (featuring such songs as "Try to Remember" and "Soon It's Gonna Rain"), is a romantic, theatrical tale of two crafty fathers who conspire to bring their children, Matt and Luisa, together—which they do.

Time and Place: Ever the present, always the hopeful place of the heart.

The Scene: Luisa (sixteen) speaks of the awakening wonder of life.

• • •

This morning a bird woke me up.
It was a lark or a peacock,
Or something like that.
Some strange sort of bird that I'd never heard.
And I said "hello."
And it vanished: flew away.
The very minute that I said "hello."
It was mysterious
So do you know what I did?
I went over to my mirror
And brushed my hair two hundred times
Without stopping.
And as I was brushing it,
My hair turned gold!
No, honestly! Gold!
And then red.
And then sort of a deep blue when the sun hit it.
I'm sixteen years old,
And every day something happens to me.

I don't know what to make of it.
When I get up in the morning to get dressed,
I can tell:
Something's different.
I like to touch my eyelids
Because they're never quite the same.
Oh! Oh! Oh!
I hug myself till my arms turn blue,
Then I close my eyes and I cry and cry
Till the tears come down
And I taste them. Ah!
I love to taste my tears!
I am special.
I am special.
Please, God, please—
Don't let me be normal!

Full Moon
by Reynolds Price

The Play: Kerney Bascomb (nineteen) attempts to find direction to her life and reconcile her relationship with a young man (Kipple Patrick), complicated by his long-standing involvement with Ora Lee, the daughter of his family's housekeeper. Issues of race and gender inform and deepen Kerney's choices while the adults around her offer advice and reflections from the past.

Time and Place: Late summer, 1938. Eastern North Carolina.

The Scene: Kerney has returned home from her date with Kipple, very late and a bit intoxicated. Finding her father still awake, their talk leads to Kerney's passionate plea for her independent womanhood, and her reluctance to marry.

• • •

KERNEY: I'm really not pregnant and I know you're a man but help—me—please. *(Real tears.)*
> *[(John rises in place, takes a step toward her. Kerney waves him back. He comes anyhow, lays a white handkerchief in her lap, touches the crown of her head for five seconds, then returns to his chair. She dries her eyes and strains for composure.)]*

KERNEY: I'm a little bit drunk. I'm not expecting, Pa—that's the truth, not a baby at least. *(Waits.)* I'm waiting—*waiting*—for life to start. *(Shakes her head.)* These last two years have been one *held* breath. See, I didn't understand that school was a *job.* It kept me busy as a bee in clover. And I got steady praise, which was better than pay. But now I feel like a Russian princess under house arrest with pernicious anemia. Not going *nowhere*, not learning a thing a chimpanzee couldn't learn in a day. Who wants to hole up with a big bunch of girls just *parked* for four years, waiting till some boy jumps their engine and drives to the altar? This is not about you. It's me, me, me. And all I'm doing is lounging around on the doorstep of marriage till some boy, that doesn't quite turn my stomach, pops the question and I say "Why not?" It's rough on my behind. Sitting here, by the year, just sitting. I've improved my mind to the point it could almost invent electricity if Ben Franklin hadn't. See, once Mother died, nobody made me want to be a woman. Nobody showed me that being a wife and mother was something a girl ought to learn.

The Scene: Kerney, facing pressure from all sides to make a decision to marry Kipple or not, attempts to sort out her feelings in front of the insisting Kipple, and both of their fathers.

• • •

KERNEY: I'm definitely *not* supposed to be here. I ought to be cool in some theater, crocheting hard and waiting for the man fate has in store. I've not failed to notice how many fine girls wait sixty years and then croak single in a nephew's back room, on charity. That would suit me fine—if I had something grand to do meanwhile, like tall white sculpture or fine true poems that'd have people bawling and set them straight. But I'm not that smart. *(Back at the steps, waits.)* Mr. Patrick if all this is coming at you from the blue and you keel over, then excuse me.

[FRANK: Kerney, believe me—my life is not threatened by any of this. I know Kip loves you and has asked for your hand.]

KERNEY: *(Waits.)* My "hand"—if I could just unplug it and turn it over, things would sure-God be a lot easier for all. But being me, I've got to go through it the hardest way, with all the human beings involved hanging on for dear life and some falling off—

[KIP: *(Gently.)* This really is your and my business. Why worry our fathers?]

[(She has no ready answer but seems relieved.)]

[FRANK: Easy, son. The lady's barely started.]

[(Kerney looks to her father.)]

[JOHN: *(Slowly nods.)* Go right on, sweetheart. Get it out of your system.]

KERNEY: Kip, I'm inventing a whole new procedure. But in a town as small as this, everybody knows we're testing each other. So ever since we parted last night, I've felt like we ought to sit down now with our two best people and think this through the only right way—if there is a way.

[KIP: *(Slowly.)* Long as everybody knows we're no way bound by majority rules.

[JOHN: Absolutely.]

[FRANK: Agreed.]

[(They all look to Kerney. She returns to the porch and sits on the railing, though farther from the men.)]

KERNEY: I'm scared as hell—excuse me. *(Waits.)* See, Kip and I know everything but my answer. He thinks he loves me and I do him. Neither one of us loves all the other one's past; we're working on that. *(Kip tries to hush her with a secret look; she nods and continues.)* But see, not having a mother to watch, I got me a powerful taste for freedom and owing nobody—nothing—never. Then I woke up at sixteen and finally heard what the world was saying—I was a girl and must act according. That meant being smart as an infantry general but keeping it the darkest secret in town. So I've toed the line through more than one beau, as they steamed up and offered me diamonds—this is not a brag. It was easy to laugh out loud in their faces. But here came Kip; Kip turned out different— *(Waits, uncertain.)*

Hekabe

by Euripides,
translated and adapted by Timberlake Wertenbaker

The Play: Euripides fifth century B.C. telling of the grief-ravaged Queen of Troy, Hecuba (Gk. Hekabe), and her revenge for the murder of her son, Polydorus. The plot draws on the classical tales of the Trojan War, and the characters of Odysseus, Agamemnon, and others.

Time and Place: The shores of Thrace, 1184 B.C.

The Scene: Odysseus has arrived to take Hecuba's daughter, Polyxena, away in order to sacrifice her to the ghost of Achilles, who has becalmed the ships of the Greeks returning from the Trojan War. Hecuba beseeches her daughter to fall upon her knees and beg for mercy but Polyxena refuses. Note: See The Trojan Women *and related Greek myths for a full appreciation of this work.*

• • •

POLYXENA: I have been watching you, Odysseus: hiding your right hand under your cloak, turning your face away to ensure I can't touch your cheek or make any other embarrassing gesture of supplication: Supplication you might have to obey. You needn't be so frightened: You will not have to answer to the god of supplication, not on my behalf at least. I will follow you of my own accord, Odysseus. I want to come with you. I want to die. For were I not content to die, I would think myself beneath contempt, a woman clinging with shameful lust to the shreds of her life. Why should I want to live? I, whose father ruled the whole of Troy. I was nurtured in the sweetness of great hopes: bred to be the bride of Kings. Indeed, the cause of no small rivalries between suitors as to whose hearth and home I should grace. I ruled over the women of Troy. And when I stood among the girls of my country, it was I who drew everyone's gaze, equal to the gods, only subject to death. Today, now: a slave. The name itself makes me long for death. I will not get used to it. And then: these questions: Who will be my master, me, the sister of Hector, and of so many other great Trojan warriors? Perhaps a man who revels in cruelty. He could force me into the kitchens, to bake the bread for the household, or to sweep his house, or make me sit with other slaves at the loom, bowed under the heavy weight of painful hours, dripping away the minutes in humiliating drudgery. And finally, some other slave, bought cheap in a market, would be ordered to come to me and soil my bed. I who was once deemed a bride fit for the greatest rulers. No. No. Freedom. Free, I relinquish this light and, free, I assign this body to Hades. And so you may take me, Odysseus. Mother, don't resist, not a word, not a gesture, help me to accept death before I suffer indignity. The one who is not used to submitting to evils bows his head eventually, but at what cost. Death is the happier course, for where there is no honour, there misery lies in wait.

Laura Dennis

by Horton Foote

The Play: Laura Dennis (seventeen) has lived with Lena Abernathy since the passing of her father. Laura has never been acquainted with her mother, as the mother abandoned the family when Laura was an infant and has since remarried and lives in South Dakota. As Laura faces the prospects of her adult life, she longs to understand the details that make up the history of her family, a history that ultimately unfolds with tragic consequences.

Time and Place: 1938. The fictitious small town of Harrison, Texas, on the Gulf Coast.

The Scene: *Laura sits with Lena on the front porch. While Laura waits daily for a letter from her mother (which will never come), rumors abound that a local boy has impregnated one of Laura's schoolmates.*

• • •

LAURA: Did you go by the post office today?

  [LENA: Yes, I did.]

LAURA: No letter for me?

  [LENA: No. Of course, there is another delivery at four o'clock.]

LAURA: You never get any out of town mail in the four o'clock delivery. To tell you the truth I don't know how I'll feel if my mother does write me and says come on to South Dakota. I'll be torn, I tell you that, because I won't like leaving you, and yet… I want to see my mother, I want to be with my mother, maybe even live with my mother. I guess what I really want is my mother to want me. *(A pause.)* I wouldn't want to live with my Aunt and Uncle even if they asked me to live with them, because I know my father didn't want me ever living out there again, and, too, because I feel in my heart my Aunt and Uncle don't really want me out there. Then, too, I want you to know that if I hear from my mother and she wants me to come to South Dakota, I'll probably go, but I'll feel sorry, very sorry to be leaving you, because I don't know what my daddy and I would have done if we hadn't been living here when he got so sick. *(A pause.)* Do you think my mother will answer my letter?

[LENA: I hope so. *(A pause.)*]

LAURA: Harvey Griswold came back to school today, but none of the girls would speak to him. Even some of the boys wouldn't talk to him. Pud says her mother heard if Harvey didn't stop telling everybody in town who will listen to him that the baby wasn't his Mr. Nelson is going to kill him. *(A pause.)* I wonder what would have happened if my father hadn't killed his cousin, and if my mother hadn't fallen in love with his cousin. His name was Harold wasn't it?

[LENA: Yes, I believe so.]

LAURA: Harold Dennis. Did you ever see him?

[LENA: Not that I remember.]

LAURA: I went to see Catherine Lacy again yesterday. She said she hears from my mother every once in a while and I wanted to know if she had heard from my mother and if she had, had my mother mentioned getting a letter from me. She hadn't heard from her, she said.

The Scene: *The last scene in the play, in which Laura's world collapses. Harvey, the young man Laura cared for very much, has been killed. Laura has subsequently learned that Harvey was, in fact, her stepbrother. She has also learned that her long lost mother has asked that Laura no longer attempt to make contact. Sitting with Lena (her one true support), Laura desperately struggles to hold on by remembering the riches of her past.*

LAURA: Looks like I'm going to get to go to college if I want to. To tell you the truth I don't know what I want. *(A pause.)* My uncle wants me to go to Sophie Newcomb. My aunt went there, he said. *(A pause.)* He said my mother got in touch with him. She asked him to ask me not to write her anymore. She doesn't want to see me. She wants to forget about everything that happened here. She's married again now and has a family. A boy six and a girl four.

(Music from the dance can be heard.)

LAURA: Hear the music from the dance? I bet they're having a good time. *(A pause.)* I saw Stewart this afternoon as he came out of the jail. I think he had been to see Mr. Nelson. He didn't see me. Somebody said he's not going back to school here, that he's going to finish out the year at Allen Academy. *(A pause.)* Do you know I've lived here with you eleven years? I was counting them up just now. When we first came to town Daddy got a house and a colored lady to cook for us and take care of me when he wasn't home. I remember when he came home and said there's a nice lady in town here that has rooms to rent and serves meals and will look after you when I'm away and we're going to move in there. You know I remember the first time I saw you. You were standing in the room there watching when Daddy and I drove by in his car and he said that lady standing in the door is the one that we're going to live with and then I saw Mr. Abernathy sitting on the porch and I said who is that and he said that's her husband, he's not well. I don't remember ever seeing him again. Why didn't I ever see him again? Do you realize if my mother walked into this yard right now, I wouldn't know her. She would have to say Laura Dennis, I'm your mother, before I'd know who she was. *(A pause.)* I went to school with my brother for I don't know how many years and I didn't know who he was and he didn't know who I was. *(She is crying.)*

Medea

by Christopher Durang and Wendy Wasserstein

The Play: A sketch written for the Juilliard School's Drama Division's twenty-fifth anniversary, April, 1994. The subject draws on Euripides' tragedy, *The Trojan Women.*

Time and Place: The stage of a drama school. The present.

The Scene: The actress playing Medea comes to introduce the evening.

• • •

ACTRESS: Hello. I am she who will be Medea. That is, I shall play the heroine from that famous Greek tragedy by Euripides for you. I attended a first-rate School of Dramatic Arts. At this wonderful school, I had classical training, which means we start at the very beginning, a very good place to start. Greek tragedy. How many of you in the audience have ever acted in Greek tragedy? How many of your lives are Greek tragedy? Is Olympia Dukakis here this evening? As an actress who studied the classics, one of the first things you learn in drama school is that there are more roles for men than for women. This is a wonderful thing to learn because it is true of the real world as well. Except for *Thelma and Louise.* At drama school, in order to compensate for this problem, the women every year got to act in either *The Trojan Women* or *The House of Bernardo Alba.* This prepared us for bit parts in *Designing Women* and *Little House on the Prairie.* Although these shows are canceled now, and we have nothing to do. Tonight, we would like to present to you a selection from one of the most famous Greek tragedies ever written, *The Trojan Women.* Our scene is directed by Michael Cacoyannis and choreographed by June Taylor. And now, translated from the Greek by George Stephanoulous, here is a scene from this terrifying tragedy.

The Merchant of Venice
by William Shakespeare

The Play: Antonio, a Venetian merchant, assists his friend Bassanio in wooing the beautiful young heiress, Portia. Antonio's good intentions land him in debt to the moneylender Shylock, however. When Shylock attempts to collect his interest payment of a pound of flesh Portia successfully defends Antonio disguised as a judge, and all ends happily except for Shylock.

Time and Place: Venice, Italy. Circa 1596.

__The Scene:__ In the following speech (I, ii) we meet Portia for the first time as she considers the strengths and weaknesses of her various suitors.

• • •

PORTIA: By my troth, Nerissa, my little body is aweary of this great world.

If to do were as easy as to know what were good to do, chapels had been churches, and poor men's cottages princes' palaces. It is a good divine that follows his own instructions; I can easier teach twenty what were good to be done than to be one of the twenty to follow mine own teaching. The brain may devise laws for the blood, but a hot temper leaps o'er a cold decree; such a hare is madness the youth to skip o'er the meshes of good counsel the cripple. But this reasoning is not in the fashion to choose me a husband. O me, the word 'choose'! I may neither choose who I would nor refuse who I dislike, so is the will of a living daughter curbed by the will of a dead father. Is it not hard, Nerissa, that I cannot choose one, nor refuse none?

[NERISSA: First, there is the Neapolitan prince.]

PORTIA: Ay, that's a colt indeed, for he doth nothing but talk of his horse, and he makes it a great appropriation to his own good parts that he can shoe him himself. I am much afeared my lady his mother played false with a smith.

[NERISSA: Then is there the County Palatine.]

PORTIA: He doth nothing but frown—as who should say, 'An you will not have me, choose!' he hears merry tales and smiles not; I fear he will prove the weeping philosopher when he grows old, being so full of unmannerly sadness in his youth. I had rather be married to a death's-head with a bone in his mouth than to either of these. God defend me from these two!

[NERISSA: The French lord, Monsieur Le Bon?]

PORTIA: God made him, and therefore let him pass for a man. In truth, I know it is a sin to be a mocker, but he—why he hath a horse better than the Neapolitan's, a better bad habit of frowning than the Count Palatine; he is every man in no man. If a throstle sing, he falls straight a-cap'ring; he will fence with his own shadow. If I should marry him, I should marry twenty husbands. If he would despise me, I would forgive him; for if he love me to madness, I shall never requite him.

[NERISSA: Then to Falconbridge, the young baron of England?]

PORTIA: You know I say nothing to him, for he understands not me, nor I him. He hath neither Latin, French, nor Italian; and you will come into the court and swear that I have a poor pennyworth in the English. He is a proper man's picture, but alas! who can converse with a dumb-show? How oddly he is suited! I think he bought his doublet in Italy, his round hose in France, his bonnet in Germany, and his behaviour everywhere.

[NERISSA: The Scottish lord, his neighbor?]

PORTIA: That he hath a neighborly charity in him, for he borrowed a box of the ear of the Englishman and swore he would pay him again when he was able. I think the Frenchman became his surety and sealed under for another.

[NERISSA: The young German, the Duke of Saxony's nephew?]

PORTIA: Very vilely in the morning when he is sober, and most vilely in the afternoon when he is drunk. When he is best he is a little worse than a man, and when he is worst he is littler better than a beast. An the worst fall that ever fell, I hope I shall make shift to go without him.

I pray thee set a deep glass of Rhenish wine on the contrary casket, for if the devil be within that temptation without, I know he will choose it. I will do anything, Nerissa, ere I will be married to a sponge.

If I live to be as old as Sibylla, I will die as chaste as Diana unless I be obtained by the manner of my father's will. I am glad this parcel of wooers are so reasonable, for there is not one among them but I dote on his very absence; and I pray God grant them a fair departure.

The Scene: In the second speech (III, ii), Portia longs for Bassanio to select the right casket and so win her hand in marriage.

• • •

PORTIA: If you do love me, you will find me out.
Nerissa and the rest, stand all aloof.
Let music sound while he doth make his choice;
Then if he lose he makes a swanlike end,
Fading in music. That the comparison
May stand more proper, my eye shall be the stream
And wat'ry deathbed for him. He may win;
And what is music then? Then music is
Even as the flourish when true subjects bow
To a new-crownèd monarch. Such it is
As are those dulcet sounds in break of day
That creep into the dreaming bridegroom's ear
And summon him to marriage. Now he goes,

With no less presence but with much more love
Than young Alcides when he did redeem
The virgin tribute paid by howling Troy
To the sea monster. I stand for sacrifice;
The rest aloof are the Dardanian wives,
With blearèd visages come forth to view
The issue of th' exploit. Go, Hercules!
Live thou, I live. With much, much more dismay
I view the fight than thou that mak'st the fray.

Molly Bailey's Travelling Family Circus

With Scenes from The Life of Mother Jones
Book and Lyrics by Megan Terry
Music by JoAnn Metcalf

The Play: Megan Terry's adventurous and magical circus telling of a fictional meeting and the life stories of two celebrated women at the turn of the century is played out by a happy company of theatricals. Mollie Baily sets the stage in the first scene of the play as she describes the Mollie Bailey-Mother Jones, "...[the] history of two mothers, mothering the miners and the countryside, working every night and every day for motherhood, and sisterhood and brotherhood and The Union of the Workers, and the Union of Heaven with this beautiful Earth..." Part history, part magic, part fable, part fact but all passion, the play brings a band of players and musicians together to present an extraordinary theater event.

Time and Place: The early 1900s—A circus arena in an unnamed location.

The Scene: Birda (young lady), one of Mollie's children is alone on stage with her horse (played by one of the ensemble actors), trying to teach the horse to dance.

• • •

BIRDA: I can walk, and you can walk. I can tie my shoelaces, and I know for certain that I can tell the time my dear, my beautiful beast. How I love my beast. I love you. I love your shining coat, and your eyes melt my heart. I was so embarrassed for so long beast, you know I only pretended to be able to tell the time. Yes, there's a beast, oh how beautiful you will be when you know all the steps, yes, there's my beast. Oh my beast you have a beautiful way of bowing on the beat. I want to fly with you. Just you learn to dance and then we will sneak away just you and I and we'll go out to the lush green bayous down by the river, and I'll bathe the sweat off your beautiful strong and perfect backside. Oh you do have a marvelous bottom my beast. I adore your magnificent and monarchly head but I have to tell you how I also adore your behind. Yes, there's a beast, that's my beast, my beast is beautiful, my beast is a beauty. Yes, raise your foot again my beauty, just ever so such a shade higher, yes, my beauty. I love you to do it that way. Yes, my beauty, you make me proud. My heart is flying, go back to the beginning my perfection and then, right, right, yes there's my beauty. How grand you will be in your harness, I'll make you the most shining and perfect, and you know between you and me, you are the true star of my circus. Yes, there's my—no, no, darling, go back, you've nearly got it, yes again, again, perfect. *(Hugs horse passionately, throws herself up on horse's back, throws down her training whip.)* Now we'll gallop all the way out to the cliffs above the river and we'll fly right off and up into the sky. We'll fly, we'll fly…

Mud

By Maria Irene Fornes

The Play: The story of three rural characters in the mud of life attempting to find human connections: Mae, a "spirited, single-minded" young woman (mid-twenties); Lloyd, a "simple and good-hearted young man" (mid-twenties); and Henry, a big man (mid-fifties) with a "sense of dignity who can barely read." Their relationships are visceral, earthy, and fundamental.

Time and Place: A house on a rural promontory. The present.

The Scene: Mae tells Henry about the nature of her relationship with Lloyd.

• • •

MAE: *(Sitting on the right facing front.)* What can I do, Henry, I don't want you to be offended. There's nothing I can do and there's nothing you can do and there is nothing Lloyd can do. He's always been here, since he was little. My dad brought him in. He said that Lloyd was a good boy and that he could keep me company. He said he was old and tired and he didn't understand what a young person like me was like. That he had no patience left and he was weary of life and he had no more desire to make things work. He didn't want to listen to me talk and he felt sorry to see me sad and lonely. He didn't want to be mean to me, but he didn't have the patience. He was sick. My dad was good but he was sad and hopeless and when my mom died he went to hell with himself. He got sick and died and he left Lloyd here and Lloyd and I took care of each other. I don't know what we are. We are related but I don't know what to call it. We are not brother and sister. We are like animals who grow up together and mate. We were mates till you came here, but not since then. I could not be his mate again, not while you are here. I am not an animal. I care about things, Henry, I do. I know some things that I never learned. It's just that I don't know what they are. I cannot grasp them. *(She goes on her knees as her left shoulder leans on the corner of the table.)* I don't want to live like a dog. *(Pause.)* Lloyd is good, Henry. And this is his home. *(Pause. She looks up.)* When you came here I thought heaven had come to this place, and I still feel so. How can there be offense here for you?

The Nature and Purpose of the Universe
by Christopher Durang

The Play: This absurdly comic play revolves around the life of the Manns. The family is headed by Steve, a religious fanatic, and held together by the beleaguered mother, Eleanor. Colorfully rounding out the family are three sons: Donald, a pimp and dope peddler; Andy, a flamboyant homosexual, and Gary, the victim of a threshing accident that has left his penis little more than a stub. Into all this comes, among others, Elaine, masquerading as Sister Annie De Maupassant, the radical nun of Bernardsville. The assassination of the new Pope is the result of these characters' interactions.

Time and Place: Kitchen of the Mann house. An ordinary Tuesday morning.

The Scene: *Elaine challenges Mrs. Mann's perceptions of her sons.*

• • •

ELAINE: *(Shouting.)* You phony liar. Your oldest son pushes dope and is a pimp. I have here a signed affidavit from three hundred badly used women. *(She takes out the paper.)* And your second son is a homosexual. I have Super 8 film of him. *(She takes out a roll of film.)* And your youngest son lost his penis in a reaping accident and I have here a signed statement attesting to that fact from the entire eighth-grade girls' gym class. So don't try to fool me with your pathetic lies. Admit that you lead a lousy life. Do you know on a national scale of one to eight hundred, you rank ninety-second; and on a local scale you are thirty-three, and on an international scale one-hundred-six, and on an all-white scale twenty-three, and on an all-black scale six-hundred-forty, and on a pink scale sixteen, and that your capability ranking places you in the lowest percentile in the entire universe? It's a sad life I see before me, Mrs. Mann. You haven't any friends. None. Do you realize that you never call anybody up and that nobody ever calls you up? And that you're universally snubbed and pitied at PTA cocktail parties? And that your husband married you only because he had to, and your housekeeping is among the most slovenly on the eastern seaboard, and your physical appeal is in the lower quadrangle of the pentanglical scale— and that's not very high, Mrs. Mann—and that your children rank as among the foremost failed children in the nation and are well below the national level in areas of achievement, maturity, and ethical thinking. WHY DO YOU CONTINUE LIV- ING, MRS. MANN? WHY DON'T YOU DO YOURSELF A FAVOR?

[ELEANOR: Please leave now.]

ELAINE: One more thing, Mrs. Mann. Even though you and your family are going to have to leave tonight before the Fuller Brush Man is scheduled to arrive, he isn't going to come for you anyway. But you'll never know for sure, cause you'll be gone. So long, Mrs. Mann! Enjoy Iceland!

The Scene: *This speech comes immediately after the Pope has shot and killed Andy Mann. Elaine offers some words of con- solation.*

• • •

ELAINE: [Yes. Yes. I should.] *(She stands on a table.)* Death comes to us all my brothers and sisters in Christ. It comes to the richest of us and to the poorest of us. Our days on this earth are rounded by a little sleep. On the one hand, pre- birth. On the other hand, post-death. It's six of one, half a dozen of another. The world about us is but a valley of tears, full of sorrows for the just and blessings for the unjust. But yet even in the appalling spectacle of death we can see God's face looking down on us. We can see His Great Plan. Like some great spider, God weaves an immense web in which to trap us all and then in a fit of righteous rage, He eats us. The Eucharist at last finds its just and fitting revenge. But we must not despair that we do not understand God. Rather must we rejoice in our confusion, for in our ignorance is reflected God's wisdom, in our ugliness His beauty, in our imperfections His perfections. For we are the little people of the earth, and His is the power and the glory, and never the twain shall meet. Hubb-ba, hubba-ba, hubb-ba.

One Flea Spare
by Naomi Wallace

The Play: A wealthy couple, quarantined in their home during London's historic plague, harboring a girl and a sailor. As death rages beyond their door the four lives entwine and disintegrate within.

Time and Place: 1665. A comfortable house in Axe yard, off King Street, Westminster, in London.

The Scene: *Morse (a girl of twelve) is locked in an empty room. Alone. She wears a dirty, tattered, but once fine dress. The dress is pulled up to hide her face. She wears a torn pair of boys britches under the dress. She repeats the words that her interrogator might have used earlier. This is the first scene in the play.*

• • •

MORSE: What are you doing out of your grave? *(Beat.)* What are you doing out of your grave? *(Beat.)* Speak to me.
  [*(We hear the sound of someone being slapped, but Morse remains still and does not react.)*]
MORSE: Speak to me, girl, or you'll stay here till it's know.
  [*(Another sound of a slap, harder. Morse still does not move.)*]
MORSE: What happened to the Gentleman?
  [*(Another slap.)*]
MORSE: What happened to his wife?
  [*(Another slap.)*]
MORSE: Whose blood is on your sleeve? *(Beat. Morse drops her dress down to reveal her face.)* The blood of a fish. Is on my sleeve. Because. The fish. The fish were burning in the channels. Whole schools of them on fire. And the ships sailing and their hulls plowing the dead up out of the water. And the war

had begun. The war with the Dutch had begun. *(Beat.)* It was March. No, it was later. In summer. A summer so hot vegetables stewed in their crates. The old and the sick melted like snow in the streets. At night the rats came out in twos and threes to drink the sweat from our faces. *(Beat.)* And it had finally come. *(Beat.)* The Visitation. We all went to sleep one morning and when we awoke the whole city was aglow with the fever. Sparrows fell dead from the sky into the hands of beggars. Dogs walked in the robes of dying men, slipped into the beds of their dead Masters' wives. Children were born with the beards of old men. *(Beat.)* They were locked in their own house, the two of them. All the windows, but one, nailed shut from the outside. They'd waited out their time of confinement. Three more days and they could escape. But then we came. In through the basement and across the roofs. One of us died. In that room. Two of us died. *(Beat.)* It was night. Yes. At night. He moved as though invisible. Gliding through the empty streets.

> [(Bunce, *making a fair amount of noise, tumbles into the cell, which has now become the Snelgraves' room. He stands facing into a corner.)*]

MORSE: He came in through the cellar. He thought the house was empty and so he made himself at home.

> [(Mr. and Mrs. Snelgrave *enter their bare room.)*]

MORSE: But his timing was off. Mr. and Mrs. Snelgrave caught him in the act of relieving himself into one of their finest vases.

The Scene: *Morse (a girl of twelve) sits alone on the floor.*

• • •

MORSE: *(Whispers.)* I can't. I can't remember.

    [(Sound of a slap.)]

MORSE: She smelled. Of lemons.

    [(Another slap, harder.)]

MORSE: Maybe she was my age. No. She was. Lissa was. A year younger. She had brown hair as long as a horse's tail and like cakes her dresses were. Rimmed with yellow and blues. Lissa had a fat stick that she kept in her trunk of toys and she would sneak up behind me as I swept the floors and hit me across the back. When I cried, she'd let me hold the bird that her grandfather brought home with him from India. It was a green and black bird and it could sing a melody. When I held it I could feel its tiny heart beating inside its chest.

    [(Darcy enters and stands in the shadows of the cell.)]

MORSE: Sometimes when Lissa's father scolded her she would come running to me and fling herself into my arms and weep. Her tears soaked my dirty frock. *(After some moments Morse gets to her feet and feels her dress is wet.)* Ugh. I've wet myself. *(Morse takes the dress off and casts it in the corner. She is wearing long underwear, perhaps a boy's, underneath.)* And then I got sick and Mr. Snelgrave shouted, "Plague! Plague!," but I had no tokens.

    [(Darcy takes up the dress and holds it, then exits with the dress.)]

MORSE: My teeth swelled. I vomited. I had the spotted-fever. For three days. Mrs. Snelgrave held me in her arms. *(Beat.)* That week Kabe said the pits were near overflowing. But Kabe said it wasn't only the dead that went to the pits. Some of the living went to the pits to die of grief. More than once, he said, when he tried to pull the grievers out of the pits he heard a sound like a stick snapping in their chests. Lissa's father, Mr. Braithwaite, died first. Then the mother. They died quickly. In each other's arms. From inside out they rotted. Lissa died more slowly. We were alone in the house. She said, "Hold me." Her body was covered in tokens. *(Beat.)* But it wasn't Lissa's blood that was on my sleeve. *(Beat.)* Who was alive and who was dead? In the pits their faces looked the same. Dried out by grief. And their hearts snapping in two inside their chests. Such a sound, Kabe said. Such a small, small sound, like this: *(Makes a small sound.)*

The Scene: *It is early morning. Snelgrave is tied to a chair, slumped over. When Morse enters she is wearing Snelgrave's shirt as a nightgown. She approaches him closer and closer until their faces are almost touching.*

• • •

MORSE: That wasn't a poor bird you did yesterday. It was quite good, really. *(She whistles like a bird, as he did earlier, then she picks up his hand. He is dead.)* Where did you go, Mr. Snelgrave? *(She unbuttons his shirt and checks his chest and neck.)* You haven't even got the tokens. *(She whistles again.)* Sir Braithwaite's daughter had a bird. A green and black bird. Whack, whack went her stick on my back when I swept. Then she'd let me hold the bird so I'd stop crying. The bird had a song like a long, long spoon and we could sip at it like jam. And the song put a butterfly inside our mouths and it opened its wings in there and made us laugh. *(Beat.)* But everyone died in that house. And then Lissa was dying too and we were alone and she lay on the floor with the tokens shining black on her neck. The tokens would not break and run and Lissa wept from the pain. She said "Hold me." *(Beat.)* She could no longer see and was blind. *(Beat.)* She said "Hold me" and I said "Give me your dress." She couldn't take it off because she was too weak so I undressed her. Lissa said "Hold me now." She was small and thin without her dress. I said "Give me your shoes" and she let me have them. I put on the dress and the shoes. I went to the looking glass. The silk of the dress lapped at my skin. The ruffles whispered hush, hush as I walked. Lissa said "Hold me, Morse. I'm so cold." I went to her then. *(Beat.)* But then she was. Dead. I sat beside her, holding the bird. It sang for her. It sang for hours and hours until its heart stopped in my hands. *(Beat.)* It was Lissa's bird. I could take her dress and shoes but I couldn't take the bird. Even dead, it was Lissa's bird. Not mine. *(Beat.)* I opened her mouth and put the bird inside. *(Morse touches Snelgrave's face.)* You are dead. I can hold you. *(She gently embraces his body.)*

Real Women Have Curves

by Josefina Lopez

The Play: The story of Ana (eighteen), a Latina living in East Los Angeles, who dreams of getting out of the barrio to get a good education and become a successful writer. In the meantime, stuck working in a small sewing factory, Ana chronicles her observations of the lives, loves and dreams of her coworkers, five heavy-set Mexican-American women.

Time and Place: The first week of September, 1987. A tiny sewing factory in East Los Angeles.

The Scene: The very last moment in the play, Ana reflects on what she has learned since leaving home.

• • •

ANA: I always took their work for granted, to be simple and unimportant. I was not proud to be working there at the beginning. I was only glad to know that because I was educated, I wasn't going to end up like them. I was going to be better than them. And I wanted to show them how much smarter and liberated I was. I was going to teach them about the women's liberation movement, about sexual liberation and all the things a so-called educated American woman knows. But in their subtle ways they taught me about resistance. About a battle no one was fighting for them except themselves. About the loneliness of being women in a country that looks down on us for being mothers and submissive wives. With their work that seems simple and unimportant, they are fighting… Perhaps the greatest thing I learned from them is that women are powerful, especially when working together… As for me, well, I settled for a secondhand typewriter and I wrote an essay on my experience and I was awarded a fellowship. So I went to New York and was a starving writer for some time before I went to New York University. When I came back the plans for making the boutique were no longer a dream, but a reality. *(Ana picks up a beautiful designer jacket and puts it on.)* Because I now wear original designs from Estela Garcia's boutique, "Real Women Have Curves."

The Reincarnation of Jaime Brown

by Lynne Alvarez

The Play: The separate quests of a young New York street poet seeking fame and fortune, and a wealthy entrepreneur who will stop at nothing to find his son who committed suicide nineteen years before, collide with astrological proportions, helped by a mystical and androgynous couple.

Time and Place: The present in New York City and the Hamptons.

The Scene: *This is the first scene in the play, in which we find Jaime (nineteen) selling her poetry in New York City's Port Authority Bus Terminal.*

• • •

JAIME: Construction in New York's a bitch. *(She passes a donut stand, hands the vendor a sheet of paper and grabs a donut. He starts to protest.)* Don't sweat it, man—in a couple of years that'll be worth a fortune. I sign all my copies. A small investment now could set you up for life, you know what I mean? *(People pass, she tries to sell them a poem.)* You want a poem, Miss…uh you there, Miss, how about a poem? Thanks a lot. And you sir…a poem, an adventure—

> *[(The man stops and looks her up and down lasciviously. Opens his raincoat and flashes Jamie. Jamie confronts him. As she walks forward, he walks back until at some point he turns and flees.)]*

JAIME: …not that kind of adventure, man, but thanks for sharing. I bet you and I are thinking alot of the same things right now. I'm out here selling poetry, but you're walking around naked under that raincoat with the same question burning between your…ah…ears.

"What's happened to poetry in America?"

Am I right?
I mean when was the last time a poem
rattled your bones?
Well here I am to remedy that.
Cast off, blast off
I'm the new wave poetry slave
I know what you're thinking—you have to study Elizabethan
English to read poetry; you have to buy an arcane insane eso-
teric totally prosaic literary magazine available in only one
bookstore on 47th street twice a year—am I correct?
Or you feel to hear a good poem you have to kneel at the
knees of some MMP—Major Male Poet preferably facing his
crotch.
Now tell me if that isn't true? Sad isn't it?
Well I say, no way
I give you your poetry straight
no rap, no rock, bee bop or hip hop
So how about five dollars, man?
You can afford it. Think of what you must save on clothes.
   [(The Flasher turns and runs.)]
JAIME: Yes, yes, yes
I'm the new wave poetry slave
the last living purist in America—
   *[(David walks by with an instrument case. She looks him
   over.)]*
JAIME: Well maybe I'm not all that pure,
Hey you—superdude.
Yeah you. What's up? *(She follows him.)*
You want a poem? A touch of culture, a touch of class
Love'em and leave'em right?
I have something just for you…
A road poem, a heartbreak poem, lonesome sexy blues.
   [DAVID: Are you trying to pick my pocket?]
JAMIE: Dude, those jeans are so tight
no one could pick your pocket without a surgical instrument.
Looks good though. Don't get me wrong.

Now, how about a poem?

I'm in a difficult profession here.

I'm a major if undiscovered poet

reduced to selling original works of art on the street.

I have hundreds of poems ready made—for all occasions,

every mood, theory, relationship and philosophy of life.

Only two dollars. Five dollars will get you

an original, custom—composed on the spot, stirring, moving unique

work of art and for only one dollar—and this is an introductory offer. I can write you a limerick as effective as a quick kick in the butt.

[DAVID: Sorry, kid.]

JAIME: Signed. Dated, limited copy.

Think of it as an investment.

Or if you like, you can pass it off as your own.

You take the credit, I'll take the cash.

No problem.

Sally's Gone, She Left Her Name
by Russell Davis

The Play: The story of seventeen-year-old Sally Decker and her parents, Henry and Cynthia, and Christopher, her brother. Mom and Dad are not what they used to be, nor is the family; life is changing—nothing seems connected anymore.

Time and Place: Summer. The present. A large kitchen in a suburban home.

The Scene: *Sally speaks of her restlessness to her mother.*

• • •

SALLY: I don't want you to wait, Mom. You're too restless to wait. [You are. I know you are.] Mom, it's not so bad to be restless. It's good. I get restless too. Mom, I do. Cause I don't want to be with Bruce, or argue with Dad. I don't want to be like us. I want something more. I want what Grandpa had. I want how he painted. Like his girl. I want to be the girl Grandpa painted. More than anything I know I want to be in that picture. Something like that picture. I want to wear that wide headband she's got around her head. And that T-shirt, I want that extra large T-shirt that's so light you can see through it. I want to go running like that in the middle of the night, more than anything I know, faraway from anybody, any town, any teachers, family. Just run up and down, visit the ocean, and the mountains, everything. Yeah. Because I think if I could do that, be some kind of little girl spirit all over again, if I could do that, and not miss all the stuff, everything in my life, the people, the things to do, then I would be happy. I could be happy in a way that I could walk around for sixty years or so until I died, wearing nothing but this white T-shirt and a headband. Except on the headband, I've embroidered:

"Sally's gone." That's right. Sally's gone. And she left her name, so don't try calling after her. She left her name.

The Scene: *Sally tells Christopher, her brother, how difficult it is to say what we mean.*

• • •

SALLY: Chris, everyone says corny stuff in private. In particular, me. Chris, I say things in my head, hopes, stuff like that, that sound just awful when I say them out loud. I've tried it. Doesn't sound at all like it did when I just thought it. It's the same with everybody. The same, I bet. Cause there's some kind of background music inside your head. I don't mean there's music, Chris, but something. Because, if I say in my head, for example, I love you, Christopher, there's a background music. Otherwise how could I say it? And I can get goosebumps on my arms from thinking about you, Christopher. I can. But if I actually said to you, I love you, Christopher, or if I said, I'm sorry. I'm sorry I made what happened to Mom. I never meant what happened to Mom. I don't know how I got so angry to make what happened.
[SALLY: I'm sorry.]
SALLY: If I said that, immediately I would feel phoney. And you too. Cause something's awkward and we'd have to argue right away to make up and get back to normal. And I don't understand how come. How come the longer you stay in this world, the longer you see everything going on, the harder and harder it gets to say what you mean. Or why you have to keep it all in your head. The older you get, the more and more stuff you have to keep in your head, any kind of hopes you ever had about living, all of it, never speaking, and it gets sicker and sicker inside your head, until you can't hold it up anymore, and you're ashamed, and you fall over, get old, and die.

Shelter

by Jayne Anne Phillips

The Story: Jayne Anne Phillips novel recounts the experiences of a group of girls at a West Virginia camp in July of 1963. Two sisters, Lenny and Alma, confront life-transforming events, tucked away in a forest-dense wilderness, away from the normal influences of an urban world. The startling and moving coming-of-age story is seen through youthful eyes. Phillips' strikingly vivid and rich prose speaks to all of the senses, sharpened by adolescent perception.

Time and Place: July, 1963. A girl's camp in West Virginia.

The Scene: This is the first page of the novel. Although the speaker is not identified, this could be the view of any of the girls who spend this hot July away at camp.

• • •

Concede the heat of noon in summer camps. The quarters wavering in bottled heat, cots lined up in the big dark rooms that are pitch black if you walk in out of the sun. Black, quiet, empty, and the screen door banging shut three times behind you. Allowed in alone only if you are faint. Perhaps the heat has come over you, settled in from above and sucked your insides until you must lie down to sleep in the empty cabin while the rest are at hiking or canoes or archery. Now you lie there sleeping and the room is heavy and warm, but cooler than noon, the rough wooden walls exuding shade. The cots are precisely mute. Identical and different in olive-green blankets, each pulled tight and tucked. In your mind, you see the bodies lying there, each in its own future. You are frightened because it is you here with the future. And they are scattered along Mud River walk, obscured by dense leaves, their occasional cries no louder than the sounds of the invisible birds.

Or they are standing in line before bright targets stretched across baled hay. They are holding taut bows straight out, pulling back on the strings with all their strength.

Spring Dance

by Horton Foote

The Play: The attendants of this spring dance are not members of the local community, but rather the patients of a sanitarium, a collection of souls crushed by their inability to exist in the real world. Although the normalcy of an evening dance is a pleasure for most people, here it brings about struggle among these patients, as they attempt to reach for a sane lifeline. At the center of the play is Annie Gayle Long, a young woman who over a period of years has lost her grip on life. Finally her family could no longer handle her situation and has sent her to this sanitarium where she is surrounded by other lost souls.

Time and Place: Spring, 1928. Austin, Texas.

The Scene: A section of enclosed garden adjoining a ballroom-auditorium where a dance is being held. Annie Gayle Long (early twenties) sits on a bench listening to the music. After a few moments, Annie notices that Dave (early twenties) has fallen asleep.

• • •

ANNIE: Don't go to sleep on me, Dave. Please, please, Dave. *(She shakes him. He wakes up.)* Let's talk. Did you read your Mother's letter? It was very interesting. Mr. Henry Vaughn died at sixty-eight. That came as a shock. Or was that in the letter? Maybe it was in another letter. Laura Vaughn is expecting her first child. She is my very best friend. But there is one thing in that letter that is not true, and you must write her at once and tell her. My husband, Mr. Long, is not remarrying. That's quite impossible, because he is still married to me. Will you write and explain that to your Mother? And if you don't, please give me permission to write for you, for I'm sure she did not mean it unkindly, and I'm sure she would be the first to want such a story corrected. *(A pause.)* Dave, how long have you been here? *(A pause, as if she expected Dave to answer. He doesn't, of course.)* I told Cecil you have been here five years, and that would make you twenty-three—wouldn't it? *(Again she waits for an answer, before continuing.)* Oh, yes. Because I remember distinctly you came here at eighteen. But what is confusing me, is that I just this instant remembered that yesterday was your birthday, and someone, maybe Greene, said that you were now twenty-eight. And if that is so, and you came here at eighteen, you have been here ten years instead of five. *(A pause.)* How long have I been here? I told Cecil two. Or is it four? Have I been here four years instead of two? If it's four my little girl was three when I left, so she would be five and he would be four. If... *(A pause.)* This is what makes me nervous, extremely nervous. I try to keep everything straight and clear. But then these doubts begin and I don't remember anything correctly. Not how long you have been here, or I have been here.

The Scene: *Annie has taken Dave's letter from his mother. Annie likes to read Dave's letters from home to hear the news of the people she misses.*

• • •

ANNIE: When was this letter written? *(A pause.)* When was it written? *(A pause.)* There is no date on it. *(A pause.)* I forget so much.

[GREENE: And I forget...]

ANNIE: But you know, I felt a certain suspicion even as I was reading the letter that I had heard this before. That's encouraging isn't it? You remember Dave in discussing the letter with you and it's news I was not sure if I had read about Mr.

Henry Vaughn in this letter or another letter. It was in this letter, but still I felt, somehow I may have heard it before, so when you said to me Mr. Henry Vaughn has been dead a year. It wasn't a total surprise. That's encouraging isn't it? *(A pause.)* There is a lot I don't want to remember, of course. *(A pause.)* But I do remember all the same. *(A pause. She looks at them.)* Mr. Long and I are divorced. I remember that now. They told me at Christmas. Mama and brother told me when he didn't come to Christmas dinner. They sent the children for a walk with the nurse, and they told me. But which Christmas was it? Was it this Christmas, or last Christmas or, the one before? I remember, whichever Christmas it was, she told me we had been divorced for six months. My mother has the custody of the children. She is their legal guardian. She insisted on that, she said, before consenting to the divorce. *(A pause.)* Then I suppose it is true Mr. Long is marrying again, and there will be no need, Dave, to write your mother to correct the rumor, *(A pause.)* but if that is written last March then I suppose he is married already. *(A pause. To Greene.)* Mr. Long was my husband. I don't suppose you ever met him. I forget how long we were married. He was always, always, always, very kind to me and very patient... I met him in Houston. We had gone there to live after the death of my Father...

Dave, I wonder if Laura Vaughn's baby was a boy or a girl? I must write and tell her how happy I am for her. She waited quite awhile before she was finally married. She went to Mexico on a two-month trip, with her cousin Laura Weems, the year I was married. Laura Weems has never married. And some people think she never will. I surely hope you find a nice girl some day Dave, and when you're feeling better, you will marry and have children. I'd be lost without my children. *(A pause. She opens her purse and gets another note.)* I want you to take this note with you tomorrow and promise me you'll give it to your mother and ask her please to see that my mother gets it. I know that my mother has not been receiving my messages. *(Dave makes no move to take the note. She doesn't press it on him. Annie, reading the note.)* My dearest mother and brother: I want to come home and see my children. I know I shall be better and not be nervous if I can only do that. *(She looks at Dave.)* I miss my children. How long have I been gone? *(She folds the note up and puts it in her purse again.)*

The Tears of My Sister

by Horton Foote

The Play: Originally written for live television, Foote's short play is seen through the eyes of Cecilia Monroe, a young lady living with her mother and older sister in a boardinghouse. For the live television production, Cecilia was only a voice and the camera served as Cecilia's eyes, moving among the actors as the character would. The story concerns Cecilia's sister, Bessie, who is promised to an older man with means, but loves another. Cecilia tells the audience her inner thoughts as the drama plays out.

Time and Place: Late summer, 1923. Harrison, Texas.

The Scene: Cecilia (a girl) is seated on the front porch of the boardinghouse. Bessie, Cecilia's older sister has just come onto the porch. Cecilia speaks to us.

• • •

CECILIA: I swear, I think my sister Bessie is the prettiest thing on the face of this earth. Mama agrees with me. But Bessie just laughs when you tell her that.

[(Bessie smells the other rose and smiles to herself. She looks as if she knew some wonderful secret.)]

CECILIA: I swanny. My sister Bessie laughs at the drop of a hat. She laughed when she failed the sixth grade, she laughed when Mama couldn't afford to buy her a new dress for the dance last winter. Of course, she cried when our cat got poisoned and when Papa died two years ago. Why, she cried then like her heart would break and would never mend in this world.

[(A pause. Bessie walks up and down the porch strumming the uke.)]

CECILIA: Of course, I cried then and Mama did, goodness

knows. But not like Bessie. Bessie cried for six months. She still cries when you mention Papa's name. I don't know why she was cryin' last night though. Nobody mentioned Papa's name to her in the middle of the night, certainly. It's all very mysterious to me anyway. Mama has forbidden me to talk to her about Bessie's cryin' in the night this way or anything until supper time. Mama says I talk too much. *(She looks at Mr. Williford and then at Miss Sarah.)* I wish I could talk to someone about it. There's so much I don't understand. Mama says she puts it all down to happiness. I wish I could go along with that.

[(Bessie puts the uke down. She smells the roses.)]

CECILIA: Bessie ought to be happy. Certainly she's engaged to a lovely man and he's so rich you just can't imagine it. So maybe Bessie is cryin' for happiness. I don't know. Now you take me. I've got plenty to cry about if I put my mind to it. I'll be lucky, Mama says, to get any kind of a husband. Much less a rich one. Oh, well.

The Scene: *Near the end of the play, Bessie has been asked to put a stop to her affections for the young Syd Carr and to marry Stacey Davis (an older man who could take care of the family and find a home). Crushed with the fate life has handed her, Bessie weeps in her room as her mother consoles her. In her room, which she shares with Bessie, Cecilia listens.*

• • •

CECILIA: Oh, I can't sleep. Mama and Bessie are in Mama's room. They've been talkin' for nearly two hours.

[(Bessie comes out of her mother's room. She looks at Cecilia's bed, decides she's asleep and walks across the room to her own bed. Mr. Williford can be heard snoring down the hall.)]

CECILIA: Now Mr. Williford has started his snorin' again. *(Cecilia sits up in bed and looks over at her sister in her bed. Bessie has her eyes closed.)* Now Bessie's in bed and not cryin' an' that puzzles me, because the way she was cryin' in Mama's room there for a while I thought she'd be cryin' all night.

[(We hear crying in the mother's room.)]

CECILIA: Now Mama's cryin'. She cries soft like Bessie, but I can hear her and somebody ought to go in to her. *(She gets up out of bed and goes over to Bessie's bed.)* Bessie? Bessie? Are you asleep? Mama's cryin', Bessie. Wake up. Mama's cryin'. And I'm cryin', Bessie, because I'm scared. I'm scared. I'm scared. I'm scared in this old boardinghouse with Mr. Williford snorin' every night and Papa dead and you cryin' and Mama cryin'…

The Trojan Women
by Euripides

The Play: Euripides fifth century B.C. tragedy set immediately after the fall of Troy, recounts the fate of Queen Hecuba, her daughters Cassandra and Polyxena, and Andromache, widow of the Trojan hero Hector, at the hands of their Greek captors.

Time and Place: Outside the walls of the fallen city of Troy, 1184 B.C.

The Scene: Half-mad, Cassandra, who is to be taken as Agamemnon's concubine, prophesies that the indignity laid upon her will result in the fall of Agamemnon's house and great suffering for Odysseus. Note: See Hekabe *and related Greek myths for a full appreciation of this work.*

• • •

CASSANDRA: O Mother, crown my triumph with a wreath.
Be glad, for I am married to a king.
Send me to him, and if I shrink away,
drive me with violence. If Apollo lives,
my marriage shall be bloodier than Helen's.
Agamemnon, the great, the glorious lord of Greece—
I shall kill him, Mother, lay his house as low
as he laid ours, make him pay for all
he made my father suffer, brothers, and—
But no. I must not speak of that—that axe
which on my neck—on others' too—
nor of that murder of a mother.
All, all because he married me and so
pulled his own house down.
But I will show you. This town now, yes, Mother,
is happier than the Greeks. I know that I am mad,
but Mother, dearest, now, for this one time
I do not rave.

One woman they came hunting, and one love,
Helen, and men by tens of thousands died.
Their king, so wise, to get what most he hated
destroyed what most he loved,
his joy at home, his daughter killing her
for a brother's sake, to get him back a woman
who had fled because she wished—not forced to go.
And when they came to the banks of the Scamander
those thousands died. And why?
No man had moved their landmarks
or laid siege to their high-walled towns.
But those whom war took never saw their children.
No wife with gentle hands shrouded them for their grave.
They lie in a strange land. And in their homes
are sorrows, too, the very same.
Lonely women who died, old men who waited
for sons that never came—no son left to them
to make the offering at their graves.
That was the glorious victory they won.
But we—we Trojans died to save our people,
no glory greater. All those the spear slew,
friends bore them home and wrapped them in their shroud
with dutiful hands. The earth of their own land
covered them. The rest, through the long days they fought,
had wife and child at hand, not like the Greeks,
whose joys were far away.
And Hector's pain—your Hector. Mother, hear me.
This is the truth: he died, the best, a hero.
Because the Greeks came, he died thus.
Had they stayed home, we never would have known him.
This truth stands firm: The wise will fly from war.
But if war comes, to die well is to win
the victor's crown.
The only shame is not to die like that.
So, Mother, do not pity Troy,
or me upon my bridal bed.

Vieux Carre

by Tennessee Williams

The Play: "The Writer," a character in *Vieux Carre* fashioned after Mr. Williams, brings us into the world of a dilapidated rooming house in New Orleans' French Quarter. Part player and part narrator, The Writer reflects on the past by reliving that past. The collection of troubled souls that occupy the rooming house form a bizarre tapestry: a brash and desperate landlady, a well-bred young lady having a steamy relationship with a hot strip-joint worker, two older women clinging to the last remains of their dwindling income, a painter who is slowly dying, and our writer, struggling for purpose amidst conflicting feelings. A rich mix of humor, cruelty, and poetry fuse together in the telling of this haunting story.

Tune and Place: The period between winter 1938 and spring 1939. A rooming house in the French Quarter of New Orleans.

The Scene: *In the first few moments of the play, Jane (a young woman of good breeding) has returned to the rooming house late, only to be startled by Mrs. Wire (the older landlady).*

• • •

JANE: Why, Mrs. Wire, you scared me! *(She has an elegance about her and a vulnerability.)*

[MRS. WIRE: Miss Sparks, what're you doin' out so late on the streets of the Quarter?]

JANE: Mrs. Wire, according to the luminous dial on my watch, it is only ten after twelve.

[MRS. WIRE: When I give you a room here...]

JANE: Gave me? I thought rented...

[MRS. WIRE: *(Cutting through.)* I told you]

JANE: I'm afraid I didn't take that too seriously. Not since I lived with my parents in New Rochelle, New York, before I went to college, have I been told to be in at a certain hour, and even then I had my own key and disregarded the order more often than not. However! I am going to tell you why and where I've gone tonight. I have gone to the all-night drugstore, Waterbury's, on Canal Street, to buy a spray can of Black Flag, which is an insect repellent. I took a cab there tonight and made this purchase because, Mrs. Wire, when I opened the window without a screen in my room, a cockroach, a *flying* cockroach, flew right into my face and was followed by a squadron of others. *Well!* I do not have an Oriental, a Buddhistic tolerance for certain insects, least of all a cockroach and even less a flying one. Oh, I've learned to live reluctantly with the ordinary pedestrian kind of cockroach, but to have one fly directly into my face almost gave me convulsions! Now as for the window without a screen, if a screen has not been put in that window by tomorrow, I will buy one for it myself and deduct the cost from next month's rent. *(She goes past Mrs. Wire toward the steps.)*

[MRS. WIRE: Hold on a minute, young lady. When you took your room here, you gave your name as Miss Sparks. Now is that young fellow that's living up there with you Mr. Sparks, and if so why did you register as Miss instead of Mrs.?]

JANE: I'm sure you've known for some time that I'm sharing my room with a young man, whose name is not Mr. Sparks, whose name is Tye McCool. And if that offends your moral scruples—well—sometimes it offends mine, too.

A Voice of My Own

by Elinor Jones

The Play: Through the voices of some of history's most amazing women authors, this collected script stands as a stunning testimony to women through all time, featuring both the contributions and struggles women have faced. The title is taken in part from Virginia Woolf's *A Room of One's Own,* a writer of astonishing brilliance who made great strides for female writers in a world dominated by men. The cast of voices ranges from the earliest (Sappho, c. 600 B.C.) to Lillian Hellman (1905–1984).

Time and Place: Today. An unnamed place.

The Scene: *Charlotte Bronte (1816–1855) explains the restlessness that consumed her life.*

• • •

CHARLOTTE: *(Crossing center.)* Sometimes I used to go up on the roof of the house and look out over the distant view. Then I longed for a power of vision which might overpass that limit; which might reach the busy world, towns, regions full of life I had heard of but never seen. Then I desired more of practical experience than I possessed; more of intercourse with my kind, of acquaintance with a variety of characters than was here within my reach. Who blames me? Many, no doubt, and I shall be called discontented. I could not help it. The restlessness was in my nature. It agitated me to pain sometimes. It is vain to say that human beings ought to be satisfied with tranquillity. They must have action. And they will make it if they cannot find it. Women are supposed to be very calm generally. But women feel just as men feel. They need exercise for their faculties and a field for their efforts as much as their brothers do. They suffer from too rigid a restraint, too absolute a stagnation, precisely as men would suffer. And it is narrow-minded to say that they ought to confine themselves to making puddings and knitting stockings, to playing on the piano and embroidering bags. It is thoughtless to condemn them, or laugh at them if they seek to do more or learn more than custom has pronounced necessary for their sex.

The Scene: *Jane Austen (1775–1817) sits at the breakfast table discussing the latest events in her life with her sister, Cassandra.*

• • •

AUSTEN: Saturday morning…here I am, my dearest Cassandra, seated in the breakfast, dining, sitting room. Having half an hour before breakfast, I will give you an account of the last few days. Where shall I begin? Which of all my important nothings shall I tell you first? Mr. Richard Harvey is going to be married, but as it is a great secret and only known to half the neighborhood, you must not mention it. Mrs. Hall was brought to bed yesterday of a dead child some weeks before she expected, owing to a fright. I suppose she happened, unawares, to look at her husband. Going to Mr. Spence's yesterday afternoon was a sad business and cost us many tears. Lizzie has had no teeth taken out, but he finds them in a very bad state. There is a very sad hole between two of her front teeth. At the ball last evening there were twenty dances and I danced them all and without any fatigue. I saw Mrs. Blount there. She appeared exactly as she did in September…with the same broad face, white shoes, pink husband and fat neck. I met a Mr. Gould. He is a very young man, just entered Oxford, wears spectacles and has heard that "Evelina" was written by Dr. Johnson! I am much obliged to you for your inquiries about my own darling *Pride And Prejudice*. No, indeed, I am never too busy to think of it. I can no more forget it than a mother can forget her sucking child. Miss Blackford dined with us on the very day copies of the book arrived from London, and in the evening I read half the first volume to her. She was amused, and really does seem to admire Elizabeth Bennett. I must confess that I think her as delightful a character as ever appeared in print, and how I shall be able to tolerate those who do not like her I do not know. Now I will try and write something else. Pray remember me to everybody who does *not* inquire after me. With best love to all your agreeable inmates. Very affectionately, J. Austen.

Monologues
for
Young Men

. . .

Albert's Bridge

by Tom Stoppard

The Play: This one-act stage play/radio play centers on Albert, a philosophy graduate, and bridge painter who succeeds in replacing all of the other painters and making the bridge his. Eventually a would-be suicide and fourteen other painters interfere with his life.

Time and Place: A big girded railway bridge. The present.

The Scene: Albert paints, observes, and comments on his world.

• • •

Dip-brush-slap-slide-slick, and once again, dip, brush, slap—oh, it goes on so nicely…tickle it into the corner, there, behind the rivet… No one will see that from the ground; I could cheat up here. But I'd know; so dip, brush, slap, slide and once again for the last time till the next time—every surface sleek, renewed—dip, brush, slap, slick, tickle, and wipe—right in there with the old rustproof rust-brown—all glossed and even, end to end—the last touch—perfection!

Simplicity—so…contained; neat; your bargain with the world, your wages, your time, your energy, your property, everything you took out and everything you put in, the bargain that has carried you this far—all contained there in ten layers of paint, accounted for. Now that's something; to keep track of everything you put into the kitty, to have it lie there, under your eye, fixed and immediate—there are no consequences to a coat of paint. That's more than you can say for a factory man; his bits and pieces scatter, grow wheels, disintegrate, change colour, join up in new forms, which he doesn't know anything about. In short, he doesn't know what he's done, to whom.

One bridge—freshly painted—a million tons of iron thrown across the bay—rust-brown and even to the last lick—spick and span, rustproofed, weather-resistant—perfect!
Dip brush, dip brush
without end, come rain or shine;
A fine way to spend my time.
My life is set out for me,
the future traced in brown,
my past measured in silver;
how absurd, how sublime
(don't look down)
to climb and clamber in a giant frame;
dip brush, dip brush, slick, slide wipe
and again.
  (Painting stops.)
I straddle a sort of overflowing gutter on which bathtub boats push up and down... The banks are littered with various bricks, kiddiblocks with windows; dinky toys move through the gaps, dodged by moving dots that have no colour; under my feet the Triang train thunders across the Meccano, and the minibrick estates straggle up over the hill in neat rows with paintbox gardens. It's the most expensive toy-town in the store—the detail is remarkable. But fragile. I tremble for it, half expecting some petulant pampered child to step over the hill and kick the whole thing to bits with her Startrite sandals.
  (Painting.)
Don't look down,
the dots are looking up.
Don't wave, don't fall, tumbling down a
telescope, diminishing to a dot.
In eight years who will I be?
Not me.
I'll be assimilated then,
the honest working man, father of three—
you've seen him around,

content in his obscurity, come to terms with public truths,
digging the garden of a council house
in what is now my Sunday suit.
I'm okay for fifty years, with any luck;
I can see my climb
up a silver bridge to paint it for the seventh time,
keeping track of my life spent in painting in the colour of my
track:
above it all.
How sublime
(Dip brush, dip brush.) Silvering the brown.
Which dot is mine?
Don't wave, don't look down.
Don't fall.

Progress. Two lines of silver meeting in an angle bracket—
and tickle in there behind the rivet—slip slop and wipe and
on we go up the slope. Does the town look up? Do they all
gawp and say to each other, look at him! How ridiculous he
looks up there, so small, how laughably inadequate. Or do
they say, How brave! One man against the elements! Pitted
against so much! The lone explorer feeling his way between
the iron crevasses, tacked against the sky by his boots and fin-
gers. Dots, bricks, and beetles. I could drown them in my spit.
Listen…
The hot sun makes you think of insects,
but this insect hum is the whole city
caught in a seashell…
All conversation is hidden there,
among motors, coughing fits, applause,
screams. Laughter, feet on the stairs,
secretaries typing to dictation,
radios delivering the cricket scores,
tapes running, wheels turning, mills grinding,
chips frying, lavatories flushing, lovers sighing,
the mayor blowing his nose.
All audible life in the vibration

of a hairdryer in the room below.
   (Painting.)
Dip brush, slide, stroke,
it goes on as smooth and shiny
as my sweat. I itch.
Paint on my arm,
silver paint on my brown arm;
it could be part of the bridge.
   (Painting stops.)
Listen. The note of Clufton is B flat.
The whole world could be the same.
Look down. Is it a fact
that all the dots have names?

Amulets Against the Dragon Forces
by Paul Zindel

The Play: A sensitive yet biting play that uncovers a complex story of a shy teenage boy forced to follow his mother, a practical nurse, from household to household as she nurses dying patients. Circumstances lead Chris (sixteen) and his mother to look after the dying mother of Floyd, a dockworker who drinks heavily and is a match for Chris's blunt and efficient overprotective mother.

Time and Place: 1995. Staten Island.

The Scene: *Chris attempts to convince Harold (late teens) to run off with him to see his father in Florida. As Harold resists the idea, Chris appeals to him.*

• • •

CHRIS: That's how your whole life should be. One adventure after another. Stanley Kusben, a friend of mine in Civics class, hitched thousands of miles and sent me postcards about turning over in a '49 Ford and seeing God in a dentist's office in Boca Raton. He had a cavity and went to a dentist who gave him nitrous oxide gas—and he pressed this ball in his hand to get a really good dose—it controlled the flow of the gas—and when he went under he said he found himself in a labyrinth, and when he looked down one hallway, he saw God running around the corner, so he ran after God, but then God disappeared around another corner, and he ran after him again, but God disappeared around the next corner and the next and the next! And when Stanley finally came to, he said he was punching the dentist and dental assistant—and they said he had exhibited the most violent behavior they had ever seen except for one housewife who had taken gas and reexperienced the pain of childbirth. Stanley said it was the most thrilling adventure he'd ever had!

Arcadia
by Tom Stoppard

The Play: Moving back and forth between the nineteenth and twentieth centuries, Arcadia examines the nature of truth and time and the contrast between Classical and Romantic sensibilities, among other issues.

Time and Place: A room on the garden front of a large country estate in Derbyshire, England. April, 1809.

The Scene: In the speech below, which follows Thomasina's speech in the section for women, the tutor, Septimus, reassures his pupil that learning and discovery is a lifelong process, and that although mankind has lost many ancient manuscripts, we must glean from those we have.

• • •

SEPTIMUS: By counting our stock. Seven plays from Aeschylus, seven from Sophocles, *nineteen* from Euripides, my lady! You should no more grieve for the rest than for a buckle lost from your first shoe, or for your lesson book which will be lost when you are old. We shed as we pick up, like travellers who must carry everything in their arms, and what we let fall will be picked up by those behind. The procession is very long and life is very short. We die on the march. But there is nothing outside the march so nothing can be lost to it. The missing plays of Sophocles will turn up piece by piece, or be written again in another language. Ancient cures for diseases will reveal themselves once more. Mathematical discoveries glimpsed and lost to view will have their time again. You do not suppose, my lady, that if all of Archimedes had been hiding in the great library of Alexandria, we would be at a loss for a corkscrew? I have no doubt that the improved steam-driven heat-engine which puts Mr. Noakes into an ecstasy that he and it and the modern age should all coincide, was described on papyrus. Steam and brass were not invented in Glasgow. Now, where are we? Let me see if I can attempt a free translation for you. At Harrow I was better at this than Lord Byron. *(He takes the piece of paper from her and scrutinizes it, testing one or two Latin phrases speculatively before committing himself.)* Yes—'The barge she sat in, like a burnished throne...burned on the water...the—something—the poop was beaten gold, purple the sails, and—what's this?—oh yes,—so perfumed that—

[THOMASINA: *(Catching on and furious.)* Cheat!]

SEPTIMUS: *(Imperturbably.)* "—the winds were lovesick with them..."

[THOMASINA: Cheat!]

SEPTIMUS: "...the oars were silver which to the tune of flutes kept stroke..."

[THOMASINA: *(Jumping to her feet.)* Cheat! Cheat! Cheat!]

SEPTIMUS: *(As though it were too easy to make the effort worthwhile.)* "...and made the water which they beat to follow faster, as *amorous* of their strokes. For her own person, it beggared all description—she did lie in her pavilion—"

Balm in Gilead
by Lanford Wilson

The Play: *Balm in Gilead* is a kaleidoscopic slice of life that centers on Joe and Darlene, who have some hope of escaping the ugly world they have fallen into among the drug addicts, pimps, and petty criminals of New York's upper Broadway.

Time and Place: The late sixties; the entire action is set in an all-night coffee shop on New York's upper Broadway.

The Scene: Dopey, a drug pusher, speaks of the human need, on whatever level, to be cared for.

• • •

DOPEY: What he's saying—about renting rooms and all—see— well, there's no reason for it but when a girl—or around here anyway most of the girls have a guy that—kinna looks after them. After all, it's a rough neighborhood; but that's not the only way he looks after them, if you follow my meaning. And the girl sorta keeps him. The guys that are lucky. He lives up in the room—sleeps in the day and the girl uses the room at night. Maybe you think they're being exploited—the girls, I mean, because they don't get ahead. Every dime goes to the john—that's the fellow. And he eventually pulls out—runs off with it—after he's stashed it in a savings account somewhere. But these girls aren't getting so much exploited because they need these guys. No one's forcing them. One leaves, then right after they get over it they're out looking for someone else. Only someone *better.* You know? Like Ann is probably half expecting her john—this guy's name's Sam, or Sammy: She's half expecting him to leave. He's been around seven or eight months; that's about par for Ann. (*Pause.*) Well, it's because they want someone around and because ·after all balling with old men all the time can get to be a drag—of course not all of their scores are old men. They get just as many good-looking guys; young fellows; high school kids and like that, they pay. Well, maybe you don't like to hear that but they do. So it's not that they get sick of the old men all the time. But these guys that they ball, they aren't—around. You know? They aren't *around.* They want probably to know someone probably. See they're—well. And they don't get new things! I mean these girls don't go out and get themselves dresses and jewelry and things. I mean they get things, but not for themselves, see; for the guy who's with them. New clothes and rings and stuff—all kinds of crap and well because it's no kind of a lark crawling in and out of bed all night and in the morning they maybe want someone who won't leave, see. Won't get up and take off. *(Very quick.)* And then they buy these guys things so the guys around can see how they keep their johns in luxury, you know. *(Pause.)* It's natural as anything. They want someone familiar. You know—to know somebody's touch or their manner or like the texture of his skin. Even if the guy's still asleep in the morning. You can picture it. And this usually keeps them from getting much else. That's what he's trying to tell her only she'll know after a while anyway because it's just a natural thing. So she'll find it out anyway but not till she's there herself.

The Scene: Dopey, a drug pusher, lashes out at the ubiquitous cockroach.

• • •

DOPEY: A roach's *attitude* just gripes the hell out of me. But what burns me, I've been reading up, not recently, but I saw it somewhere where not only was the roach—that same, exact, goddamn roach that we know—not only were they around about two million years before man, you know, before we came along: Anthropologists or whatever, geologists over in Egypt or somewhere, looking for the first city, they dug down through a city, and straight on down through another, you know, they're piled up like a sandwich or in layers like a seven-layer cake. And they cut down, down through one century to the one before it and the one before that, and every one they found more goddamned cockroaches than anything, and they got before man ever existed and like in the basement of the whole works, there those damn bugs still were, so they've been around, like I said for about a million years before we came along. But not only that! They've made tests, and they found out that a roach can stand—if there was going to be a big atom explosion, they can stand something like *fourteen times* as much radio-whatever-it-is, you-know-activity as we can. So after every man, woman, and child is wiped out and gone, like you imagine, those same goddamn cockroaches will be still crawling around happy as you please over the ruins of everything. Now the picture of that really gripes my ass.

A Bird of Prey

by Jim Grimsley

The Play: A modern tragedy set in a large city in California where the young people face good and evil on their own terms, with calamitous consequences. When Monty's dysfunctional family moves to a complex urban environment from rural Louisiana, Monty attempts to find genuine faith, while at the same time struggling to shield his younger siblings from the temptation and danger they encounter everywhere.

Time and Place: The 1990s. An Unnamed City.

The Scene: *We see Corvette (teen) who has recently been killed at the hands of a sexual predator and left in a shallow grave. As the lights rise, Corvette faces the audience. There are many wounds on his body, cuts and burns. Also on stage are the Street Angels, three young angels who had also died in their youth.*

• • •

CORVETTE: It's not very comfortable, lying here. The dirt is cold, especially underneath. The dirt on my face gets a little bit warm sometimes and I think it must be daytime, there must be sunlight But underneath me it's cold, and kind of wet, with things crawling around. *(Pause.)* Maybe you think I shouldn't talk about this, maybe you think you shouldn't have to listen. Kids get killed all the time, what's the big deal? *(Laughs.)* Kids really do get killed all the time. I should know. *(Pause.)* We're supposed to have this happy childhood, right? We're supposed to have loving moms and dads and safe homes and sweet neighborhoods and life is supposed to be clean and nice and everything, all soft rugs and good furniture and nothing bad ever happens, right? That's us. That's who we are. We are the kids, the next generation, and nothing is supposed to touch us. And when we're little our moms and our dads can still talk to us, or, well, not really talk to us but just talk, and we think everything is okay, and fine, and sweet, and nice. All day long everything is nice. But then we get older. Mom and Dad don't like us so much when we're older. When we were little we were reminding them of something, maybe of who they used to be, when they were all safe and little and happy, maybe reminding them of when they were little kids and everything was fine. But then we get older and we don't remind them of anything nice any more, and we start to get sexual and we start to want to drink the same things they drink and we don't need them so much and they don't like that, we don't stay home so much and they don't like that, and the neighborhood doesn't seem so nice and all the people in it don't seem so sweet and all the kids are older and they hang together. *(Pause.)* Anyway. It turns out to be a world where people get killed. Where kids get killed. Like I did. *(Pause.)* I mean, I already knew some kids who got killed before I did. In my neighborhood, in Glendale, these parents had their kids in a day care center and this man walked into the day care center and shot them, every one of them, and their teacher and the woman who made their lunch. She was this Spanish woman who made tacos and stuff and she didn't even speak English but he shot her. It was on the news, you heard about it, everybody heard about it. This guy shot all these kids with a semi-automatic rifle and then he shot himself, and then the police came and took pictures of all the dead kids and took the bodies away and washed away all the blood. They talked to all his friends and his friends all said he was the quiet type, he kept to himself, who knew he was a monster like that? And they talked to his mom and she said he was not a monster, he was so sweet when he was a little kid himself. *(Pause.)* They couldn't put him in jail because he was already dead so pretty soon everybody stopped talking about it except to say that it was horrible, they just couldn't understand it, and when I was alive I never thought about it very much, but now that I've been murdered too, I understand more. That's just the way things are. It's not a nice world, or a sweet world, or a good world. Mom and Dad wish it were nice and sweet and they tried to make it look like that when I was little, so no wonder they got mad at me when I started to find out that part was all a lie. It's a bloody world. It's a mean, nasty, evil world where people eat each other. All the time. *(Pause.)* No wonder parents are so crazy. No wonder kids are so crazy. Trying to pretend like that, with each other. It catches up with you. *(Pause.)* I didn't even tell you how I died, did I? *(Laughing.)* I didn't even tell you who killed me. But you'll find out.

The Scene: We find Evan (Monty's fourteen-year-old brother), alone. He faces the audience and rages about his brutal family.

• • •

EVAN: I hate them for bringing us here. I hate Mama as much as I hate Daddy, and I hate Daddy all the time. I hate him when he sits around the house in his stinking tee shirt spilling beer all over everything and throwing up in the toilet. I hate the look in Mama's eyes when I'm at home, I hate the way she hides. This place stinks and she knows it and he knows it and they act like it's going to be different someday but it never will, and they know that too, they know they're lying and we shouldn't have come here, they know it will never get better here, but they won't take us home, I know they won't, they'll just sit here, and Daddy will keep getting drunk all the time because his job stinks and Mama will keep crying because he drinks so much and because we don't have any money, and they'll fight all night and we'll have to listen, me and Monty and Marie, we'll have to lay in that stinking apartment and listen to him screaming at her and her begging him to go to sleep. Begging him not to hit her. I know. Things can never get better here, not for us. And they ought to know it and do something about it, they ought to take us home, but they won't. So I hate them almost as much as I hate this place. It's all I can feel, this ball of hate that's on fire, that's right here inside me all the time. It's all I can feel, till sometimes I wish I could just go away somewhere. Some place where I'd never have to think about anything again.

Class Action

by Brad Slaight

The Play: A collage of encounters and solos occurring outside the classroom, reveals the difficulties of coming-of-age in the complex environment of high school.

Time and Place: A year in the 1990s. Various parts of an unnamed high school.

The Scene: Dennis (teen) confesses the dilemma of life as a genius.

• • •

DENNIS: My name is Dennis Gandleman. Around this school I am the object of ridicule from most of the students, simply because I have an extremely high I.Q. It's 176. My father wanted me to enroll in a special school that deals with geniuses like myself, but Mother was firmly against that. She wanted me to have a normal education, and not be treated as some kind of freak… Which is ironic, because that's exactly what is happening to me here. The whole concept of education is a paradox: High School is supposed to celebrate education and knowledge, but what it really celebrates is social groups and popularity. In a perfect world, a kid like me would be worshipped because of my scholastic abilities, instead of someone who can throw a forty-yard touchdown pass. I suppose I could complain, and bemoan the unfairness of it all. But I am bright. I know something that the others don't… That, once we leave High School and enter the real world, all the rules change. What matters is power. Financial power. Power that comes from making a fortune on cutting-edge computer software. Software that I am already developing. *(Pause.)* Some call me a nerd. I call myself…ahead of my time. See you on the outside.

The Danube

by Maria Irene Fornes

The Play: Breaking the formula of linear realism, *The Danube* explores what Susan Sontag calls the "psychology of tortures"—in this case the ever present threat of nuclear war. Under this weight, a collection of "well-mannered working-class" characters live out a series of scenes that leads to a final flash of annihilation.

Time and Place: Budapest. Beginning in 1938, the play quickly shifts back and forth in time.

The Scene: A waiter in a small, working-class restaurant, addresses the audience in a rapid, declamatory style on the difference between the European and the American way of life.

• • •

(The Waiter speaks rapidly in a declamatory manner. Through the course of the speech he gradually raises the tray which he holds with both hands in front of him.)

WAITER: We are concerned with quality. That which is lasting. Craftsmanship. A thing of quality always ends up being heavy. We have preferred quality to anything else. We wish for things to last but we tire of them. We are buried under the stones of buildings, iron grates, heavy shoes, woolen garments, heavy sheets, foods that smell potent like the caves in the black forest. Hands that cut, knead and saw and measure and chisel and sweat into everything we see. Pots that are too heavy to use. Shoes that delay our walk. Sheets that make our sleep a slumber. Americans sleep light and wake up briskly. You create life each day. Here, the little trousers a boy wears to school are waiting for him at the store before he is born.

We are dark. Americans are bright. You crave mobility. The car. You move from city to city so as not to grow stale. You don't stay too long in a place. A person who lives too long in the same house is suspect. It's someone who is held back. Friction keeps a stone polished. Mobility. You are alert. You get in and out of cars limberly. That is your grace. Our grace is weighty. Not yours. You worship the long leg and loose hip joint. How else to jump in and out of cars. You dress light. You travel light. You are light on your feet. You are light hearted and a light heart is a pump that brings you to motion. You aim to alight, throw the load overboard. Alight the flight. You are responsible. That is not a burden. You are responsible to things that move forward. You are responsible to the young. Not so much to the old. The old do not move forward. You will find a way for the old to move forward, have them join in your thrust. Solving a problem is not a burden to you. A problem solved is a lifting of a burden. Egyptians lifted heavy stones to build monuments. You lift them to get rid of heavy stones. Get rid of them! Obstacles! You are efficient. You simplify life. Paper work. Your forms are shorter, so is your period of obligation. Work. Your hours are shorter and you have more time to sit on the lawn in your cotton trousers.

Every Seventeen Minutes the Crowd Goes Crazy!
by Paul Zindel

The Play: The lives of the children in a large family turn complex when the parents abandon them in favor of traveling the country to the trotting races and Native-American casinos. The absent parents (gone now for two months) have left no provisions and show no signs of returning, communicating only by fax machine. As the children are divided about the pluses and minuses of being parentless, the tensions mount.

Time and Place: The present. Staten Island.

The Scene: Dan (teen), one of the older brothers in the family, faces the audience and recalls a time he observed his mother (a psychotherapist) acting overly neurotic, obsessed with a current patient she was seeing.

• • •

DAN: The only thing I noticed different about my mother was the way she would sit around the house crying a lot—which, I suppose, is unusual for a psychotherapist. She seemed obsessed with the case history of this one child patient she had. She kept printing out copies of it and leaving it around our breakfast table and at the neighborhood ashrams and supermarkets. It was something horrible that had happened to a ten-year-old boy at Christmas. His parents were loaded. Filthy rich. The father was a Hollywood producer. His mother was a Mutual Funds feminist. And they wanted to surprise their son with the greatest Christmas ever—so they bought him wonderful things: a Schwinn ten-speed; rollerblades; a Lionel electric train set, skis, a sled, a tennis racket, a dog, candy, a BB pistol, a Swiss army knife—a Christmas tree flooded with gift-wrapped boxes and bows and tinsel everywhere. A huge living room crammed with presents and candy canes. They had created this dream for their son, and on Christmas morning, their son came down the stairs into the living room—this ten-year-old boy saw this fantasy they bought him—and he burst into tears! "What's the matter, son?" his father cried out, rushing to him, holding him, hugging him—"Is there something you had your heart set on that you don't see? Is there something we forgot?" And the kid, wailing through his tears said, "I don't know, but there *could* be. There *could* be!" And that was when his father took back his hand and slapped his son with all his might. He slapped him and slapped him and slapped him!

The Scene: Dave (late teens), Dan's older brother, has returned home to see his family. Here he tells Dan about the family he has been staying with.

• • •

DAVE: The house where I'm staying... It's this woman's—this family's. They've got a dog—a Springer spaniel. Her name's Mrs. Cavucci, that's the family's name... They include me in on things. Like everybody wakes up, we eat breakfast together—then someone says "Hey, let's go on a picnic"—and they grab their stuff and drive to a park. Play ball, sit on blankets, read books... They're vegetarians—Mrs. Cavucci makes cauliflower cheese pie, and this other thing we call cheese flops. Cheese flops sucks...They're liberal, the parents—but they put the kids first, they're holding double jobs to put them through college. The father pays the car insurance for his son, an old VW bug—it goes *Vroom Vroom*... At dinner they do this lame thing, we sit around the table and everyone tells one good thing that happened to them that day, and one rotten thing—and when you tell the bad thing, somebody says, "Hey, maybe I can help fix that." I don't mind hanging out there. It's sixty dollars a week. The room sucks. They've got photos all over the place. If one of the kids writes a poem, *Bam,* it gets glued up. And Mrs. Cavucci has this nun sitting on the fireplace mantle, it's really freaky, this foot tall carved nun that's holding a real inch size bible—they're not religious but they do Christmas and Hanukkah—they're like really crazy liberals. Stupid momentos all over the place... A really dumb Model T Ford sculpture that's mounted on a teaspoon. I mean a lot of crap. Mexican paintings. A candle snuffer. They've got junk we've never even thought of—but sometimes they all go out and I go upstairs—this white rug goes upstairs where their bedrooms are—quilts and worn Indian rugs all over the place, and writing desks and books... And I get dizzy. Sometimes I have to hold onto the railing, because it seems the whole house is flying through space—like it's some kind of big time capsule—a whole house hurtling through the universe on a journey—and it makes me feel I want to go with it...

A Fair Country
by Jon Robin Baitz

The Play: Spanning ten years, this hard-hitting story features a family compromised by greed and, finally, destroyed in the process. The Burgess family is living in Durban, South Africa, while the father (Harry) serves as a cultural attaché—bringing artists to South Africa to improve America's image. In an attempt to get the family out of Africa and secure a better position, Harry betrays his oldest son's (Alec) radical friends to the government. As events play through the next ten years, bitterness consumes the family, compounded by an emotionally overwrought mother, Patrice. The consequences are devastating.

Time and Place: 1977–1987. Southern Mexico; Durban, South Africa; and The Hague, Holland.

The Scene: Near the end of the play, Patrice encounters Gil (early twenties) at an archeological excavation site in Southern Mexico. Many unresolved issues exist between mother and son, particularly surrounding the horrible death of Gil's brother, Alec.

• • •

GIL: You know it was a bullet…to the back of the neck. Behind a grocery store in Soweto. I imagine it was painless. So you don't have to worry about that. *(Beat.)* I think it was a simple assassination. I was in Kenya with him a few days before, and begged him not to keep going down there. He knew there were many people, with great, vast reasons to kill him. But he kept going anyway. It reached the point where I simply could not stop him. Even Carly couldn't stop him. God knows she stuck it out. *(Beat.)* He kept going back to South Africa again and again and again. They might have just let him fade away but he wouldn't allow them. *(Beat.)* And that was that. At least in the end, he got what he wanted. *(Beat.)* I left Kenya, got to Jo'burg at four in the morning, went to their morgue, and I said "Yes. This is my brother, Alec Dalton Burgess." They gave me his stuff. And I left.

The Fantasticks

By Tom Jones and Harvey Schmidt

The Play: This, the longest running off-Broadway musical (featuring such songs as "Try to Remember" and "Soon It's Gonna Rain"), is a romantic, theatrical tale of two crafty fathers who conspire to bring their children, Matt and Luisa, together—which they do.

Time and Place: Ever the present, always the hopeful place of the heart.

The Scene: Matt (twenty) speaks of his love for Luisa.

• • •

MATT: There is this girl.
I'm nearly twenty years old.
I've studied Biology.
I've had an education.
I've been inside a lab:
Dissected violets.
I know the way things are.
I'm grown-up; stable;
Willing to conform.
I'm beyond such foolish notions,
And yet—in spite of my knowledge—
There is this girl.
She makes me young again, and foolish,
And with her I perform the impossible:
I defy Biology!
And achieve ignorance!
There are no other ears but hers to hear
the explosion of my soul! There are no other eyes but hers
to make me wise, and despite what they say of species,
there is not one plant or animal or any growing thing that
is made quite the same as she is. It's stupid, of course, I
know it. And immensely undignified, but I do love her!

The Former One-On-One Basketball Champion
by Israel Horovitz

The Play: A two-character play in which the characters attempt to settle an old score. Fourteen-year-old Irving Katz encounters Irving Allen, a former professional basketball star, on a New York City playground basketball court, and learns that Allen's son is the one who killed Katz's father during a robbery. As the short play unfolds, Allen attempts to atone for his son's actions. The game they play is almost a metaphor for the contest of life both man and boy have faced.

Time and Place: The present. A New York City playground basketball court.

The Scene: Near the end of the play, Katz (fourteen years old, small, slightly chubby) has been pushed by Allen to the breaking point.

• • •

KATZ: He was thirty-eight; fat; never even watched sports on television, let alone played them. He went to work at seven in the morning and he came home around ten at night. I'd wait up every night just to hear him say "What's'a matter with you, Irving? It's ten'a'clock and you got school t'morrow? You wanna' end up sellin' black bean soup like your father? You wanna' end up cryin' day and night like your mother?" *(Looks at Allen: smiles.)* My mother has emotional problems. She cries a lot. Since my father got shot in the neck, she only cries from seven in the morning 'til ten at night. She use'ta go 'round the clock. She's getting better *(Pauses.)* I don't wanna' end up with the black bean soup and I don't wanna' end up cryin' round the clock...and I don't wanna' end up like you. I don't like any of the choices here... *(Pauses.)* I use'ta wanna' end up like you. That's a fact.

[ALLEN: You're your own man, Irving.]

KATZ: *(Interrupting sharply.)* I'm my own birdturd. Irving! *OOOoooo!!!* How come you turned out ta' be such a nothing, huh? How come you turned out ta' be such a *whining nothin'*? *OOOOOoooooo-Ooooooo!!!* You got all the yah-tah-duh yah-tah-duh *sincere* crap look in your eyes, like I'm s'pose'ta feel *sorry for you!* Bad break, huh? Your game just sort'a fell to nothin, right? I'm s'pose'ta feel sorry for that! Your lunatic son empties a gun into my father's neck and gets to walk around the neighborhood like he's a hero and I'm some sort'a jerk for havin' no father and *you* want *me* to feel sorry that *it hurts you! (Screams.) I'M SORRYYYYYYYeeeeeee!!! (Softer.)* You bet your ass Jews are smarter. I just wish we were *taller*, that's the truth. Then we'd have it all! *ALL! (There is a short silence during which the two men look at one another. Katz breaks the silence, softly. His attitude changes.)* I wanna' finish this game now, okay? *(Throws ball to Allen.)* Your move.

[*(Allen nods. He starts out with the ball, fades to his left and intentionally knocks ball toward Katz, who catches it and tosses it back to Allen, fiercely.)*]

KATZ: Don't you ever—*ever!*—boot a ball in my direction, pal. I got my points on you *straight* and I'm gonna' beat you straight. *You...hear...me???* Shoot!

[*(Allen pauses, aims, shoots, hits.)*]

Henry IV, Part I

by William Shakespeare

The Play: The first of two histories chronicling the life and times of Henry IV and the assumption of his son, Prince Henry (Hal), to the throne as Henry V. Warring factions headed by Owen Glendower and Henry Percy (Hotspur) threaten Henry's throne. Prince Hal, who has been leading a profligate life with a band of merry men headed by "plump Jack" Falstaff, finally wins his father's respect when he helps defend the throne by killing Hotspur in battle and defeating his rebel army. (See Prince Hal's speech from *Henry IV, Part II*.)

Time and Place: England and Wales. Early 1500s.

The Scene: The fiery Hotspur (I,iii), who has recently come from battling the Scots, attempts to explain to King Henry that he has not refused to turn over the prisoners he has captured, but that the King's emissary did anger him.

• • •

HOT: My liege, I did deny no prisoners.
But I remember, when the fight was done,
When I was dry with rage and extreme toil,
Breathless and faint, leaning upon my sword,
Came there a certain lord, neat, and trimly dress'd,
Fresh as a bridegroom, and his chin new reap'd
Show'd like a stubble-land at harvest-home;
He was perfumed like a milliner;
And 'twixt his finger and his thumb he held
A pouncet-box, which ever and anon
He gave his nose and took 't away again;
Who therewith angry, when it next came there,
Took it in snuff; and still he smil'd and talk'd,
And as the soldiers bore dead bodies by,

He call'd them untaught knaves, unmannerly,
To bring a slovenly unhandsome corse
Betwixt the wind and his nobility.
With many holiday and lady terms
He questioned me; amongst the rest, demanded
My prisoners in your majesty's behalf.
I then, all smarting with my wounds being cold,
To be so pest'red with a popinjay,
Out of my grief and my impatience,
Answer'd neglectingly I know not what
He should, or he should not; for he made me mad
To see him shine so brisk and smell so sweet
And talk so like a waiting-gentlewoman
Of guns and drums and wounds—God save the mark!—
And telling me the sovereignest thing on earth
Was parmaceti for an inward bruise;
And that it was great pity so it was,
This villanous salt-petre should be digg'd
Out of the bowels of the harmless earth,
Which many a good tall fellow had destroy'd
So cowardly, and but for these vile guns,
He would himself have been a soldier.
This bald unjointed chat of his, my lord,
I answer'd indirectly, as I said;
And I beseech you, let not his report
Come current for an accusation
Betwixt my love and your high majesty.

Henry IV, Part II
by William Shakespeare

The Play: The second of two histories chronicling the life and times of Henry IV and the assumption of his son, Prince Henry (Hal), to throne as Henry V. Following the death of Hotspur and the defeat of his rebel army, new warring factions turn against Henry. Henry's forces eventually prevail and Prince Hal, who has turned from Falstaff and his dissipated followers, is crowned King Henry V upon the death of his father. (See Hotspur's speech from Henry IV, Part I.)

Time and Place: England and Wales. Early 1500s.

The Scene: Before the deathbed of King Henry (IV, v), Prince Hal honors his father and prepares himself to be king.

• • •

PRINCE: O, pardon me, my liege! but for my tears,
The moist impediments unto my speech,
I had forestall'd this dear and deep rebuke
Ere you with grief had spoke and I had heard
The course of it so far. There is your crown;
And He that wears the crown immortally
Long guard it yours! If I affect it more *[Kneels.]*
Than as your honour and as your renown,
Let me no more from this obedience rise,
Which my most inward true and duteous spirit
Teacheth, this prostrate and exterior bending.
God witness with me, when I here came in,
And found no course of breath within your majesty,
How cold it struck my heart! If I do feign,
O, let me in my present wildness die
And never live to show th' incredulous world

The noble change that I have purposed!
Coming to look on you, thinking you dead,
And dead almost, my liege, to think you were,
I spake unto this crown as having sense,
And thus upbraided it: "The care on thee depending
Hath fed upon the body of my father;
Therefore, thou best of gold art worst of gold:
Other, less fine in carat, is more precious,
Preserving life in med'cine potable;
But thou, most fine, most honour'd, most renown'd,
Hast eat thy bearer up" Thus, my most royal liege,
Accusing it, I put it on my head,
To try with it, as with an enemy
That had before my face murder'd my father
The quarrel of a true inheritor.
But if it did infect my blood with joy,
Or swell my thoughts to any strain of pride,
If any rebel or vain spirit of mine
Did with the least affection of a welcome
Give entertainment to the might of it,
Let God for ever keep it from my head
And make me as the poorest vassal is
That doth with awe and terror kneel to it!

Home Fires
by John Guare

The Play: It's the night of the day after the signing of the Armistice ending World War One and the Schmidt—"Smith"—family is trying to have the funeral for their wife and mother, recently deceased. Their attempts are thwarted when the funeral director discovers their "Germanity" and throws all the grieving mourners out. This wacky farce doesn't try to explain itself or make real sense, which is half the fun. Before the short play is over, we've seen magic and a small patriotic parade marching through the funeral home.

Time and Place: November 12, 1918. Catchpole's Funeral Parlor. A very posh establishment on Ocean Boulevard in Swampscott, Massachusetts.

The Scene: Rudy (the Schmidt's son—twenty-five years old) has returned for his mother's funeral only to find chaos. As he bonds with his father and sister, he recounts the events of his past few years.

• • •

RUDY: I'm an agent!
  [PETER: An agent?]
RUDY: I personally represent the Ben Hur Animal Stables. Till I took it over, it was the biggest dog account in the whole William Morris Agency. They gave me the account as a baptism of fire to see what I could do and, boy, christen me Big Shot because the Ben Hur Stables is now the fourth biggest account we handle right after Will Rogers, Miss Fanny Brice, and the Creole Fashion Plate. All thanks to me. I got the Met doing twelve Aïdas. That's six camels right off and they don't come cheap. The Hippodrome's got two elephants and a diving palomino that leaps right into the pool for Annette

Kellerman's finale and Mr. Ziegfeld's got six, count 'em six, white horses in his climax alone. It's been the best theater season in years! Mr. William Morris *himself* patted me right on the head—this head—and he said, "What's your name? You're going far." The breath all went out of me, Papa, and that night I got all dressed up in my white tie and tails and stood outside the Follies waiting to see my acts. I also got three afghans in the First Act finish when who comes along—I'm standing in front of the Nieuw Amsterdam Theatre—me, Rudy Smith, in my white tie, top hat, cape with a silk lining, feeling my head like it was a crystal ball and Mr. William Morris had read the future in it—and I look up and I see there's Pepper and Felix down from Lynn on the prowl and they get a look at me in my glad rags and the crowd is hurrying in to see the show and you can hear the overture out there on Forty-second Street and my boyhood chums pick up dog dirt and start throwing it at me and barking, and the carriage trade is watching and traffic is stopped and even Mr. Ziegfeld's top assistant, Goldie, comes out to see what the noise is. "Let's go sell it," Pepper keeps yelling, and Felix is in the background laughing and barking. Woof. Woof. I turned my back on them and walked into the theater just as fifty of Mr. Ziegfeld's finest twinkled and beamed and turned into naked rays of sunshine for Irving Berlin's "Fountain of Youth" number. As the audience gasped and applauded, I changed my name on that spot to Rudyard Smythe and if the applause wasn't for me, it was good enough and I said I'm never going back to Lynn till I'm something, Papa, till I'm better than dog dirt. That was two months ago and look at me, Papa! Since I changed my name, I got this wonderful girl who I'm hoping will accept my hand and my arm and all of me in the state of wedded bliss. She's so classy, Papa. Take her to Lyman Street? Oh, boy. Even Swampscott isn't good enough for her. You should see her apartment, Papa. Her bathroom alone is all red velvet. All of it. The seat, the chain.

[PETER: She must be very neat.]

RUDY: And she sleeps with her hands in dishes of cream scented with mint and rubs honey under her eyes so she won't ever get a wrinkle, and for perfume she rubs, really soft-like, Grand Marnier Brandy all over her body and the smell of it lingers so soft...

[PETER: She doesn't take a bath?]

RUDY: Papa! Three times a day! In a tub that looks like a golden swan. And the water spouts are the breasts of a China lady and the water sprays out and you turn it off by moving these gold and silver feathers. Silver for hot. Gold for cold.

[PETER: She must have a very nice job.]

RUDY: *(Transported.)* Papa, she's Anna Held's roommate! *(Sings to illustrate:)*

Every little movement has a meaning all its own,

Every little meaning has a movement all its own,

Every little movement,

Every little meaning,

Every little movement has a meaning all its own.

Anna Held, Papa! The famous Ziegfeld star and ex-wife of same and the roommate of my Margaret Ross-Hughes.

Hot 'n' Throbbing
by Paula Vogel

The Play: Perhaps in other hands, this story would seem like a common modern tale of a divorced family, coping with one another and the pangs of growing up with separated parents. In the hands of the magical Paula Vogel, the story is anything but common. A divorced mother, caring for a teenage girl and boy, makes her living writing screenplays for adult films. When the kids find out mom's true profession, it's cool. But when the father barges back into their lives (breaking a restraining order), the family disorder builds to overwhelming proportions with dark consequences.

Time and Place: The present.

The Scene: *Woman (the mother) takes a private moment with Boy (Calvin the son) to inquire about Girl's (the daughter, Lesley Ann) weekend outings with her friend Lisa.*

• • •

BOY: Well...see, first they hitch into town with some suburban-father type in his Volvo station wagon. They then hop the crosstown bus, the M2, to the corner of Pike and 7th. They get off by the bus station, and walk two blocks east. They check to make sure they're not being followed. Then they duck into this joint, it's all red brick on the front, with the windows blacked out, except for the Budweiser sign. The door is solid metal. They nod to the bouncer, who always pats Leslie Ann on the fanny. They trot behind the curtains in back of the bar, quick, see, so the clientele won't see them in their street clothes. And backstage, Al who's the owner, yells at 'em for being late.

And they slip into this toilet of a dressing room, where they strip off their jeans and sweats in such a hurry, they're inside out, thrown in the corner. And they help each other into the scanty sequins and the two-inch heels. And they slink out together in the blue light as the warm-up act, and wrap their legs around the poles. And Al keeps an eye out on the guys, who haven't got a buzz on yet, so they're pretty docile, 'cause the girls are jailbait. And Leslie Ann and her best friend Lisa shake it up for only one set. And before you know it, the twenty minutes are up, just a few half-hearted grabs, and they're doing full splits to scoop up the dollar bills that will pay for the midnight double feature at the Mall and the burgers afterwards at Big Bob's.

The Kentucky Cycle
by Robert Schenkkan

The Play: A series of nine short plays, this Pulitzer Prize–winning cycle of plays spans two centuries and seven generations of Kentuckians. The plays focus on the lives of the turbulent Rowen family as they evolve through the years, and the plays probe the myths of American expansion and growth that have produced what we are today.

Time and Place: Eastern Kentucky. 1775–1975.

The Scene: *The following speech is from the section of the play titled "God's Great Supper" that is set in 1861 on the Rowen homestead. Jed Rowen (twenties) flees his father Ezekiel's fire-and-brimstone preaching and tells of his own visions and the specter of William Clarke Quantrill, a fearless guerrilla fighter for the Southern cause.*

• • •

JED: I sneak out of church and into an apple orchard where the trees are so full of crows the branches crack under their weight. The fruit rots on the ground. The trees are all beaks and eyes and appetite. There's a cold church picnic laid out on tables underneath the trees, and I sit down and a ragged woman puts a plate of food in front of me. She goes and kneels next to her sister. I'm hungry and I eat. I eat alone 'cept for this one man who sits acrost from me, his hat pulled low so I can't see his face. I can see his hands, though, and his nails are torn and bleeding. When I finish my plate the woman brings another one. And when I finish that, another one. And then another. I eat till I am full to burstin', but I'm afraid to stop. Afraid what might happen to me if I stop eatin'. I make myself sick, and when I look up again the man removes his hat and I know him now—he's Quantrill. William Clarke Quantrill. "Have some more, Jed," Quantrill says, and he laughs. And then the women begin to speak.

The Less Than Human Club

by Timothy Mason

The Play: A troubled young man recreates a turbulent year in his life (1968) with the hopes of finding answers to paths that have led to today. The journey back replays the complexities of relationships, the crisis of sexual identity, the bonds of truthful friendship, and the search for purpose.

Time and Place: Fall of 1967; winter/spring of 1968. Minneapolis, Minnesota.

The Scene: *Davis (the central character) begins the second act of the play with the historical context of 1967 on an international level and on a personal level.*

• • •

DAVIS: *(To audience.)* By the end of 1967, there were four-hundred-eighty-six-thousand American troops in Vietnam, a disproportionate number of them poor and black. Nearly ten thousand died there that year. In October, a hundred and fifty thousand protesters marched on the Pentagon. A few of them stuck blossoms into the barrels of the soldiers' rifles. Hundreds were arrested. The race riots of the long hot summer had cooled some, but over a hundred American cities had burned and there was nobody to haul away the ashes. In January North Vietnam launched the Tet offensive, and the Green Bay Packers beat Oakland in Super Bowl II. Like I cared. I was working on the big stuff. Look—can I just skip to what I want to say? My mother's got me going to this shrink because she's afraid maybe I'm not normal. Okay, me too, maybe I'm afraid I'm maybe not normal. But I hate it! This old guy with hairs growing out of his nose and his ears, he keeps talking about his own childhood, like how hard he had it, sole support of about twenty-eight brothers and sisters, and I don't really care, you know? And about healthy thoughts and unhealthy thoughts, but Father, I hate it, I don't feel sick. I don't think I'm sick, I don't know. If I were sick, wouldn't I feel sick? I sort of want to clip the hairs on the end of his nose, maybe that's sick. But I've asked this girl to the next dance you know, and that scares me a little bit. So what I want to know is about the power of prayer and all that. You know?

Lloyd's Prayer

by Kevin Kling

The Play: Bob, the Raccoon Boy, has been raised by the raccoons, was rescued by Mom and Dad but soon after is stolen by an ex-con who sees Bob as the answer to his prayers...fame and fortune. Things go well for Lloyd until a mysterious angel (dressed like a cheerleader) comes into Bob's life and attempts to save him. This wonderful comedy plays out the ludicrous "human" selfishness that fills the world. Before the fun and games are over, Mr. Kling has done much more than make us laugh—he's challenged us to consider our shallow greediness.

Time and Place: The present. A small town in mid-America.

The Scene: The opening of the play in which we find Bob, a boy raised by raccoons, high in a tree talking to his shadow. A thunderstorm is moving in.

• • •

BOB: Hello. Hello. Don't be afraid. I'm not. Are you new here? I said, are you new here? I'm not. This used to be my home but it seems different now...smaller. I don't seem to fit anymore. What's your name? What are you, then? *(Chatters.)* I wish I could speak to you but I've forgotten how. Sorry. I have been called many things in my life but I prefer Bob. I am an orphan. I could no more tell you my real father than the ingredients to a hot dog. I do remember my mother. I remember the night she became frozen and died. I remember snuggling next to her warm coat, my brothers and sisters crowding in to get at the milk but I was the biggest so I always got a spot. I remember her dark eyes. She taught me to always wash my food. She taught me to never trust a smile because that's right before something bites. I remember her on the side of the road. She saw the lights, became frozen and died. Lloyd says it happens all the time and she probably isn't in heaven because she didn't have a southern accent. Since I was the biggest, my siblings turned to me. I remember leading them to a house for food. The large metal cans full of food, the metal trap and the sound of my arm as it broke. I remember pulling to get free, pulling on the pain. I knew I was human. I knew when I saw the trap. I was not a raccoon. I knew what I was doing. I was making a choice. I saw the trap, I saw the choice. I was human. I was human. I was human, I was trapped, and a man was running toward me with a gun. Lucky for me he was a doctor.

The Scene: *Near the end of the play Bob, a boy raised by raccoons, finds the answer to his existence.*

• • •

BOB: Angel. Angel. I need you. Hello. I know who you are now. I recognize you. You have changed. I have changed. Sometimes I feel you behind me, flat against a rock or a tree. My shadow, my darkness. I feel you most when I'm with the angel. When I stare at her like my mother with the headlights. That's when you're the strongest, when you wait. It's your purpose. You wait. I know why I am a spirit, not a human. A spirit. I have a soul...trapped. I see the trap, I see the choice. I know why you wait for me. To move on. To be with the angel. I will dive through you to the other side. Dive through your darkness and leave my shell behind and when I surface there will be light, there will be the angel. Waiting. Happy for no reason. I am a spirit. Lucky for me there's an angel who loves me.

Marco Polo Sings a Solo

by John Guare

The Play: This comedy presents a bizarre picture of the future through the lives of Stony McBride, a movie director and adopted son of a former Hollywood legend, who is developing a screenplay about Marco Polo for his father to star in. Complications develop through a wild cast of characters, such as his wife and her lover, Tom, a politician who has a cure for cancer; Stony's mother, a transsexual; and Larry, who has a set of mechanical legs—among others.

Time and Place: A galaxy of stars and an island off the coast of Norway. 1999.

The Scene: Stony sings to Tom the praises of man's "plant nature."

• • •

STONY'S VOICE: *(Up in space.)* Bolts came. I was on earth. Now I am here. I dodge quasars. I am not hallucinating. Hallucinations never bring peace. This is real. Glass of milk real. I ascend through space twisting, turning to show gravity does not apply. I am being carried home. Frank Schaeffer waits for me on the new planet. We shall re-enact some primitive conception. Become true father and son. The answer to some prophecy at last. I count the one moon we know. Two moons. Three moons. Four. Forty moons! The silver suit knows the way to its rightful owner. We pass a third moon of Venus. There it is. The new planet. I see Frank Schaeffer's little space craft on it. Sending out beeps. I land on the planet. So green.
[(We see a large green planet. We see Stony in his space suit. He calls out.)]
STONY: Hellooo?? Frank Schaeffer??? Anybody home? Am I alone on the planet? A light rain falls. I hear a music like two

crystal glasses rubbing together. I feel around. A green plant dances by, its tendrils reaching out to me. It must recognize my plant nature. I want union with this green plant. I want to set roots down here. I risk death. I take off my suit. I stand naked. I stand erect. I take the plant and hold it to me. We breathe. The plant shudders with delight. In an instant, I see little images of me run up the stem, fill up the stamen. These perfect representations of me pop out of the petals. I take another plant. That plant becomes pregnant, wrapping its leaves around me. More *mes* pop out of the petals. This is the world I want! A world populated by only me. I hear a scream. One *me* hits another *me*. Is that a rape? One of the *mes* rapes another *me?* More *mes* now march out of more petals. *Mes* fill the horizon. Downtown India is a ghost town compared to all the *mes* screaming in fear. *Me! Me!* Notice *me!* Each *me* screaming to be heard. *Me! Me!* Each *me* ignoring the other *me.* Each one moaning, whining *Me!* This is not the *me* I had planned to be. I came up here to find Frank Schaeffer. My true self. My true father. My true son. All I see are these *mes.* I take an axe. I slash the plants. I stomp on the roots. I take a gun. I shoot all the *mes.* I take flame. I burn the planet. Flames in space. I burn the new planet. I don't care. I want these *mes* out of *me.* I have killed a planet.

[(The planet turns bright red and then disappears. Stars reappear and then Earth comes into view. We no longer see Stony. We hear his voice on tape.)]

STONY'S VOICE: I put my suit on. I twist a gauge. I plunge down toward earth. Is the fear out of me? I am so quiet. I have killed me. I want no more solos. I crave duets. The joy of a trio. The harmony of a quartet. The totality of an orchestra. Home. I head for home! Duets! Trios! A quartet! Yes, even an orchestra. Make some music out of my life. I descend on my garden. I am home.

The Scene: Stony floats in space connecting with all that he is or ever has been.

• • •

STONY: Mankind's problem in a nutshell. We never go far enough. We have to keep pushing ourselves further and further to recognizing the needs of others. I recognize the needs of the grape. The grape wants to live. The veal wants to die. Why should I stand in the way of the veal? Deny the grape. So locked off from life with your peace work. Don't you know anything? Next life around, I'm coming back as a vegetable researcher. I'm committed to being an artist in this life. But it feels so inadequate when I compare the work I'm doing to the work they're doing on vegetables. Have you ever heard the cries of the asparagus? *(Stony presses a button. Agonizing screams are heard.)* Granted zucchinis are dumb. *(Moans are heard.)* But radishes are brilliant. *(More squeals.)* If we could just break the code... All the money wasted trying to break the language of the dolphin. They finally do. What are the dolphins saying to us? These high reedy squeaky voices singing "Sun goes down, Tide goes out, darkies gather round and dey all begin to shout." I have no sympathy for mammals. Meat can run away. Meat has wings. Meat has gills. Meat has hooves. Meat can escape. Meat can change. Meat can die. Meat wants to die. But plants have roots. Plants are trapped. Plants are dependent. Plants know about survival. Plants have to stay there. One of the great fallacies of science is aligning man with the mammals. Man is a plant. We may look like meat, but we're not meat. We can never escape. We can never change. We are planted firmly in the ground. We are what we grow out of. My plant nature. I celebrate that.

   [(Freydis enters with the wine and glasses.)]

STONY: Ahhhhhh, veal wine. Thank you, Freydis. You certainly have fabulous friends, darling. Tom Wintermouth himself flying up from Washington? Paris? New Zealand? Tom, why is

New Zealand bombing the hell out of Toronto? Explain New Zealand's anger? I mean, what happened to negotiations?

[TOM: Let me explain negotiations.]

(Stony suddenly breaks away from Tom. A spotlight comes down on Stony as the lights dim slightly on the stage during his speech. Stony advances to the foot of the stage.)

STONY: Frank. Schaeffer. Has. Found. The. New. Planet. He flies beyond the third moon of Venus. A green shadow blurs that part of the galaxy. This planet is on no map. A green planet so fertile it looks like a ball of manure popped out a black hole in space. Frank Schaeffer lands on the new planet. The earth will never go hungry again. He is elated. Immortality guaranteed. He toasts the plants that live on this planet with powdered champagne. One special plant dances by. Frank Schaeffer is aroused. Frank Schaeffer is lonely. Frank Schaeffer has been without contact for five years. This plant may not be human but it beckons to him, waving its leaves. Frank Schaeffer risks death. He takes off his space suit. He stands naked. He stands erect. The green plant wraps its tendrils around him. Frank Schaeffer forces the green plant down. The green plant tilts Frank over. The plant overpowers Frank. Pistils. Stamens enter Frank. Green sap spills. Bursts. I've lost contact. My head is dead.

[(The lights come back up. Diane comforts Stony.)]

STONY: I can't go into the new century this frightened.

Marvin's Room

by Scott McPherson

The Play: Bessie has committed her life to caring for others, among them her invalid father and aunt. When she discovers that she has leukemia, she is forced to contact her long-estranged sister, Lee, about the possibility of a bone-marrow transplant. Lee arrives with her two sons, Hank and Charlie, who have problems of their own, and a difficult reunion ensues. Throughout the play, Bessie meets the challenges of facing her own death, as she has always lived—by giving love to others.

Time and Place: The present. Various locations in Florida and a mental hospital in Ohio.

The Scene: Hank (seventeen) speaks to Aunt Bessie of his dreams to be free of the psychiatric hospital where he has been placed because he burned down the house.

• • •

HANK: Most of the time I keep to myself. Most of the time I sit in my room. I've got a roommate, but most of the time he's got his face to the wall. Most of the time I think about not being there. Someone I see on the TV or in a magazine, or even walking free on the grounds. They can keep me as long as they want. It's not like a prison term. I've already been there longer than most. A lot of the time I think about getting this house with all this land around it. And I'd get a bunch of dogs—not little ones you might step on but big dogs, like a horse—and I'd let them run wild. They'd never know a leash. And I'd build a go-cart track on my property. Charge people to race around on it. Those places pull in the bucks. I'd be raking it in. And nobody would know where I was. I'd be gone. Most of the time I just want to be someplace else.

Mass Appeal

by Bill C. Davis

The Play: This thoughtful, powerful, and funny play deals with the generation gap found in the priesthood. Mark Dolson, a young seminarian, comes to study and work with Father Tim Farley, an older priest who has burned out internally (his faith and his passion), but has years of experience in the showmanship of the priesthood. When young Dolson begins to call Father Farley on his sloppy, passionless, theology and on his contradictions in his life, the fire roars. Before it is over, both men learn from one another and form a bond.

Time and Place: The present. Autumn. The office of Father Tim Farley and the St. Francis Church.

The Scene: _Mark (early twenties) gives his first sermon at St. Francis. He has just been introduced to the parishioners by Father Farley with: "There's a certain James Dean quality about him which I think you'll find very exciting. Will you welcome please—Deacon Dolson."_

• • •

MARK: Thank you Father Farley. It's funny—I never stopped to think that on my way to becoming a priest I'd have to live with the name, Deacon Dolson. It sounds pretty silly, don't you think? "Deacon Dolson." _(A cough—he freezes.)_ Can I ask all of you a question? Why did you come to mass today? What brought you to church this morning? As a teenager I had a friend who answered this question by saying, "I go to mass because my parents go." But one day, I heard his father talking to my father: "Betty and I go to mass because of the kids." _(Coughs.)_ I know when I was young, I liked going to church because right after mass my father would take us to the bakery. And all four of us—my two sisters and my brother and myself—would pick out what we'd like. I'd almost always get jelly doughnuts, and I'd never wait to get home before having one... *(Coughs.)* Anyway—jelly doughnuts aren't a very good reason for going to mass, are they? *(A missal drops.)* What are your reasons... *(Coughs.)* I wonder if the coughing lot of you know, or *try* to know why you pull yourselves out of bed every Sunday morning and come here!? *(Silence.)* Do you need to come to mass? Do you need the church? Ideally, the purpose of the church is to become obsolete. But until it is, we need the habit of coming together and collectively recognizing that there is another world. There is a world that coexists and gives order to this world. Individually, we come to mass with our own personal chaos and together we look to be ordered. We must come with our hearts open for that. *(Coughs.)* But you come here with your mink hats and your cashmere coats and your blue hair—that doesn't change anything. Those things are your shackles—they are accessories you've made essential—you are essential. You come here a faceless mass—you wear your prison uniforms as if they were badges. You're slaves all week—do you want to be slaves here too...

The Scene: *After Father Farley admonishes Mark for his recent sermon, Mark defends himself.*

• • •

MARK: I know what they could be.

[TIM: But Mark—what about what they are? What are they to you?]

MARK: *(Pauses.)* They're my family. They get to me. But I don't know how to get to them. Show me.

[TIM: *(Pause.)* St. Francis got completely undressed in the middle of his town square—he gave all his clothes back to his father, and then he was ready to live. Do the same be naked—and then talk to them—as if they were one person—talk to them, as if...they were me.]

MARK: *(To Tim.)* I had a tank of tropical fish. Someone turned up the tank heater and they all boiled. *(Moving slowly to the pulpit.)* I woke up on a Friday morning—went to feed them— and there they were—all of my beautiful fish floating on the top. Most of them split in two. Others with their eyes hanging out! It looked like violence, but it was such a quiet night. And I remember wishing I had the kind of ears that could hear fish screams because they looked as if they suffered and I wanted so badly to save them. That Sunday in church, I heard that Christ told his apostles to be fishers of men. From then on, I looked at all the people in the church as fish. I was young so I saw them as beautiful tropical fish and so I knew they were all quiet screamers. Church was so quiet. And I thought everyone was boiling. And I wanted the kind of ears that could hear what they were screaming about, because I wanted to save them. *(Pause.)* A few years later, the people in the church lost the stained glass look of tropical fish, and they were only catfish to me—overdressed scavengers. So I drowned out whatever I might be able to hear. I made my world—my tank—so hot that I almost split. So now I'm back— listening—listening for the screams of angels.

The Merchant of Venice

by William Shakespeare

The Play: Antonio, a Venetian merchant, assists his friend Bassanio in wooing the beautiful young heiress, Portia. Antonio's good intentions land him in debt to the moneylender Shylock, however. When Shylock attempts to collect his interest payment of a pound of flesh, Portia successfully defends Antonio disguised as a judge, and all ends happily except for Shylock.

Time and Place: Venice, Italy. Circa 1596.

The Scene: In the speech below (V, i), Lorenzo, Bassanio's sensitive, music-loving friend, has fallen in love with Jessica, Shylock's daughter. Jessica's lines may be omitted for monologue study.

• • •

Lorenzo:
   [Sweet soul, let's in; and there expect their coming.
   And yet no matter; why should we go in?
   My friend Stephano, signify, I pray you,
   Within the house, your mistress is at hand,
   And bring your music forth into the air. *(Exit Stephano.)*]
How sweet the moonlight sleeps upon this bank!
Here will we sit and let the sounds of music
Creep in our ears; soft stillness and the night
Becomes the touches of sweet harmony.
Sit, Jessica. Look how the floor of heaven
Is thick inlaid with patens of bright gold.
There's not the smallest orb which thou behold'st
But in his motion like an angel sings,
Still quiring to the young-eyed cherubins;
Such harmony is in immortal souls,

But whilst this muddy vesture of decay
Doth grossly close it in, we cannot hear it.
    (Enter musicians.)
Come ho, and wake Diana with a hymn!
With sweetest touches pierce your mistress' ear
And draw her home with music.
    [JESSICA: I am never merry when I hear sweet music.]
    [LORENZO: The reason is, your spirits are attentive.]
For do but note a wild and wanton herd
Or race of yourthful and unhandled colts
Fetching mad bounds, bellowing and neighing loud,
Which is the hot condition of their blood:
If they but hear perchance a trumpet sound,
Or any air of music touch their ears,
You shall perceive them make a mutual stand,
Their savage eyes turned to a modest gaze
By the sweet power of music. Therefore the poet
Did feign that Orpheus drew trees, stones, and floods;
Since naught so stockish, hard, and full of rage
But music for the time doth change his nature.
The man that hath no music in himself,
Nor is not moved with concord of sweet sounds,
Is fit for treasons, stratagems, and spoils;
The motions of his spirit are dull as night,
And his affections dark as Erebus.
Let no such man be trusted. Mark the music.

Moon Under Miami

by John Guare

The Play: As with *Marco Polo Sings a Solo, Moon Under Miami* continues John Guare's assault on the "kitchen sink" drama— the kind of realistic, naturalistic drama where the audience sits observing the action through the imaginary fourth wall. Guare returns the audience to the "poetry, song, and joy" of theater by creating a new reality, which in the case of *Moon* is similar to a "savage political cartoon."

Time and Place: An iceberg. Miami. The present.

The Scene: In the play's opening monologue, Otis—is he an Eskimo?—directly addresses the audience.

• • •

OTIS: *(To audience.)* I love the way Alaska feels. You have all the dark at once. And then you have all the daylight at the same time. It's neater. The hard part of it is it is harder to shadow people. First of all, there are no shadows. Fashion wise, it's harder to trail people because everyone looks the same. But that's all democratic and good. In the Inuit—the Eskimo language—Alaska is the word for Great Land. And it is a great land. Look! A caribou leaping! I sit on an ice floe here at Point Hope and watch Russia on the horizon across the Bering Strait. To see your enemy that close. Oh, I know, I know. The evil empire is gone, but the Russians are still over there, nabbing our whale blubber, and the Federal Bureau of Investigation of which I'm an agent—Hello—Special Agent Otis Presby here—accept no substitutes—the bureau is noth- ing if not vigilant. The lesson of the caribou, mountain goats, fur seals. They are peaceful because they're vigilant. They know who their enemies are. I like an enemy. Some people say the lonely quiet must drive you crazy, but No! I have all these icebergs for company. I look at my icebergs sailing by, all grand lumbering innocence like great thoughts as yet unthought. Yes. All great ideas started out as icebergs. The wheel. Language. Love. Democracy. The Federal Bureau of Investigation. America. Each great idea began as an iceberg floating down to us, tilting, calving, melting until those ideas become part of our souls. *(Ominous music.)* And then one day an Eskimo floated by on an ice floe. Dead. And another. And another. And another. Their faces blue. Bloated. I know the Eskimos put their dead on ice floes and send them out to become part of the great—the Great Idea—but this one. I rake it in. This Eskimo is clutching in his dead fist two things. A hypodermic needle and a campaign button. "Time for a change. Vote for Reggie Kayak." He's the congressman from Eek. Is there any connection? I hold up the empty bag that had contained the Chinese cut heroin. *(Otis looks at the label.)* I can't read the label in this light. Only the chlorine blue light of the iceberg. Wait. The death dealing snow has a label. A street name. It says "Moon Under Miami."

[(A trio of Mermaid Voices sing:)]

[MERMAIDS: *(Offstage.)* A new kind of moon…"]

OTIS: *(To audience.)* It's Friday afternoon. I follow the congressman from Eek. He's in a panic. I call his office, pretending to be the telephone repairman. "Is the congressman from Eek there? He's making an emergency trip out of town? Thank you." Hmmm. Won't let him out of my sight. I have frequent flyer miles. Be back at my post on Monday. Nobody will know I'm gone. What can go wrong?

Only You
by Timothy Mason

The Play: Big-city life and complex labors of love find this group of young people trying to sort out each others' problems—with little success. Everyone's expectations are beyond any realistic reach, and the attempts are deliciously funny.

Tune and Place: The present. A large metropolitan city.

The Scene: Bo (twenties) is having coffee with Miriam (also twenties) in a local coffee shop, divulging his self-esteem issues.

• • •

BO: "Two cappuccini," God. I wish I were classy, but I don't have the background for it. I don't have the background for anything. I don't have a background. It's like I was found in a handbag or something. A background like that doesn't prepare you for the challenges of life. Take anything. Take interpersonal relationships. I don't have any. I talk, but no one listens. It makes you wonder if you're really there. I get the urge to go to the restroom and check myself out in the mirror, but I don't dare. What if I don't see anything? You know the kind of person I'm talking about? No class, no background, no interpersonal relationships? It's like the kind of person who is destined to end up working in an orthopedics appliance shop. I should know, I work in one. I get a discount across the board so if you ever need anything... The three other guys in the shop are a lot like me. We voted to remove the mirror in the restroom. Actually, when we voted there were four abstentions, so one guy just took the thing down. It's really gonna kill those guys when I tell them about you and me, they're gonna die. Or listen. Better yet. Come by the shop. Just drop by. Say you're browsing. And then, when I come out of the restroom, let your face just, like, light up. Okay, Miriam? It'll be wonderful, they'll die. Parties are usually such a letdown. For me, the saddest part of a party comes when I'm home again, taking all the unused condoms out of my pockets...and I'm asking myself why six? Bo, what did you think was going to happen? That's why I feel so special today. Here we are, just a guy and a gal in a coffeeshop, relating in an interpersonal way. You know what I mean?

The Scene: *Leo (twenties) enters his dark apartment, turns on the light, and is shocked to see Heather there. Heather has been sent by her friend Miriam (who has just broken up with Leo) to return Leo's keys. This is the final blow for Leo, the end of miserable day. Here he confesses the depth of his desperation to Heather.*

• • •

LEO: I'm ready to go. I'm ready to be translated. After today I could come back as a weasel and feel a sense of relief. We're catering this retirement party, some poor old advertising salesman on his way out, I swear every moment of the entire afternoon was written by Arthur Miller. With choreography by Dr. Joyce Brothers. I'm tending bar. The chef is, to begin with, drunk. And Hungarian. And a queen of monumental proportions. A queen for all times. This guy belongs to the ages. Do you know how to say "Please stop squeezing my buttocks" in Hungarian? They told us there'd be ice. I find the refrigerator in the employee lounge where this gala is to take place, and yes, there is ice. One tray with half a dozen cubes that smell like goat cheese. No problem. I call, I order enough ice for a hundred and fifty alcoholic advertising executives. A considerable order. And just so Eugene O'Neill doesn't feel neglected, an eighty-year-old man cometh with tongs, yes, in this day and age, tongs and a single block of ice as big as a recreational vehicle. Now I am not the sort of person who, in the normal course of events, would dream of abusing the elderly. But here is this enormous... I didn't touch him, I swear, I never laid a hand on that old man, but I'm convinced that if his heart is still beating tonight it's not my fault. This colossus of ice is sitting on the carpet in the middle of the lounge, where he dropped it, and the old man is crying, and the ice also is watering up the place a bit, and the chef is doing one of the dances of his native land. The party is due to start in six minutes. I'm chipping away at Mount Rushmore and pouring cheap white wine into plastic glasses made by some Taiwanese with a sense of humor. This is to say that every third glass has an aperture at the bottom as well as the top, and by this time I, too, am shedding tears. Approximately five minutes early the ad execs all arrive, every man-jack of them, and yes, they're thirsty. It's Wild Kingdom here, we're with the hippos at the watering hole.

This is pleasant, this is a sleigh-ride to grandma's house, this is Christmas morning when you've not been naughty but nice. All these people, the old guy who's retiring and these one hundred and forty-nine other desperate, thirsty people, what they do is they sell space. Empty space. An inch here, an inch there, half a million a page. To whom do they sell these empty inches of white paper? To the manufacturers of pain-less hair-removers for women. To the fabricators of "resort slacks." To the artisans responsible for creating souvenir china with Michael Jackson's face on every plate.

Okay. One man is called to be an Albert Schweitzer. Another hears in the drums of his destiny a sales pitch. With this I have little or no problem. But to sell empty space in order that it be filled up with nothingness is in my mind a breaking of the human bond. Okay. This is not my concern. I have sold myself, you understand, in order to fill up the sell-ers of emptiness with cheap white wine. Which in itself is nothing to crow about. Although I will say in my own defense that there is for what I am dispensing a clear and obvious need. Where am I?

The speeches! Is where I am. I'm preparing myself for incongruity here, I'm readying myself for the kind of farewell address which might be more appropriate for a Madame Curie or a Don Mattingly. I don't want to be sickened by any earnest hypocrisy, so I take a sort of psychological antibiotic as a precaution. But what I hear I am by no means prepared for. What I hear, from the Second Administrative Vice-President in Charge of Retirement Parties, leads me to believe that not only does no one in the room give a shit about this desperate old man—this is not surprising, this too I expected—but that they actually detest him. What shocks me about this valedictory is the obvious spirit of malice with which it is delivered. They all loathe the old guy. They always have. And from what little I've been able to glean from the old man's persona at the bar, they have every right. Okay. The Second Administrative V.P. announces that they've awarded the outgoing sales rep a forty-inch TV. Applause. A little limp, but people are putting their hands together. Sixteen years of selling nothing, forty inches of television, there is a kind of logic at work. Forty inches! Do you have any idea how big a forty-inch screen is? Can you imagine what a statement it would make in your living room?

Okay. It's nearly five. And as the hour approaches, the movement in the room is from eye to wristwatch. They've had forty-five minutes of Hungarian hors d'oeuvres and cheap white wine, the old asshole won't be there in the morning, and by God they're going to split. Maybe the retiree has a sense of this. Maybe he suddenly decides that having dedicated his life to selling tweezerless hair removers, he has followed an empty dream. Maybe he doesn't like the forty-inch TV. I'm not sure. But you know the sort of retirement party where the retiree pulls out a handgun and starts shooting? This was one of them. A hundred and fifty drunken advertising salesmen hit the deck. I, too, am on the floor. With the

Hungarian queen. Do not ever, I mean this, ever get down on the floor in the middle of a potential bloodbath with an iffy Hungarian.

(Sings.) "Make the—world go away…"

Men are screaming, women are screaming, crying, they're all crawling for the door, the retiree is reloading and the Hungarian is feeling me up. By this time I don't care. By this time it's taking my mind off my problems. I hope you won't get the wrong idea if I say that by this time there is something blissful about it. The bullets are whizzing above our heads, the V.P. has been winged and is not being a man about it, one of the secretaries is giving birth, and yet there's no one on earth but me and this fanatic chef. Do? You're asking me what did I do? I delivered a bouncing eight-pound baby girl, that's what I did. The jerk with the gun was moved by the sight. Said he always wanted a girl, since his sons had turned out to be such turds. This was a winning guy, I'm telling you. When the police took him away he gave me his card.

Over the Tavern

by Tom Dudzick

The Play: A two-act play about a devoutly Catholic family, the Pazinski's—Chet and Ellen and their four children, Rudy (twelve), George (thirteen), Eddie (fifteen), and Annie (sixteen). The story unfolds with great humor and love of humanity, so, despite the tribulations of daily life, hope abounds.

Time and Place: The time is autumn, 1959. The Pazinski apartment above Chet's Bar & Grill and other locales in a city somewhere in the Northeastern United States.

The Scene: Rudy, angry with his father, has just run into the sanctuary of the church; he genuflects, kneels, and challenges Jesus to give him a sign that his prayers aren't landing on deaf ears.

• • •

RUDY: *(Out of breath and sobbing.)* Jesus, I hate him, I hate him! I know I'll go to hell for saying that, but I can't help it, I do. Why does he have to be that way? You could do something, why don't you? Couldn't we have Robert Young for just one day?… Jesus, I never hear from you. I pray every night for things to get better. If you could just let me know that you're listening. A sign. Nothing big. Just something so I'll know you're working on it. Here, I'll watch that candle. *(Somewhere off in the distance.)* If you make it light up I'll know everything's going to be fine. Ready? Okay, I'm watching. Go. *(Rudy watches intently for a while. Nothing happens.)* The one on the end there. On the left. *(More watching. Nothing happens.)* Okay, I'll close my eyes. *(Hands over his eyes. Then he slowly peeks at the candle.)* Okay, you probably want to give me a better sign. I understand. Like when the angel appeared to Mary. Okay, so I'll wait. I'll wait until tomorrow morning. We had a deal, Jesus. I said I'd be a soldier for you. Please, let me know you're listening. Please. If you don't... I don't know. I guess I'll have some thinking to do.

The Scene: *Rudy back in church, this time because his prayer to make Sister Clarissa ease up on him seems to have resulted in more than he intended.*

• • •

RUDY: Boy, thanks a lot! I just asked that you make her ease up on me, I didn't say rub her out!... And now Daddy's bad mood is worse. And we never did get the spaghetti. Is this a punishment? All 'cause I'm looking for something else? How can you blame me, Jesus? All I get from you is rules. No miracles, no fun, just rules. And *crazy* rules! Like don't eat meat on Friday. I can't believe you came all the way down to Earth to say that. What's it for? Eddie says you might've done it for the Apostles, to help their fish business. That I could see. But, okay, they're dead now, and I'm still eating fish sticks on Friday. And I hate fish sticks! And other stuff, like giving up things for Lent. Last year, because you died on the cross, I gave up TV for a month. I'm not complaining. But in the end you came back from the dead, and I saw everything on reruns anyway, so what was the point?... I've got to keep looking, Jesus. But you understand. I know this kid, Arnie Silverman; I always see him at the Sunday matinees. And he says you switched religions, too. You started out Jewish! And you said it yourself—"Go thou and do likewise!"

A Prayer for My Daughter

by Thomas Babe

The Play: After the murder of an old woman, two suspects are hauled into the police station for questioning—Sean, a middle-aged homosexual, and Jimmy, his street-urchin friend who's on drugs. Throughout the grueling interrogation we learn much about the predicaments and traumas of the accusers and the accused.

Time and Place: A squad room of a downtown precinct. The present.

The Scene: In the course of the action, Jimmy has gotten hold of one of the officer's guns. Now he forces them to listen, closely, to his story.

• • •

JIMMY: *(Enraged.)* I wanna say something and if you don't go over there and sit down, I mean, like now, I'm gonna blow your fuckin' brains out. I mean it. All right, I said to myself, "Jimmy, sweetheart, you may haul dog-do for the rest of your life, and uphill, but you and this woman of yours, blown up like a balloon, you've both come to this sacred place and you are about to have a son." Well, I was, you can laugh, but I was going to, and she thought so, too, she said, "I'm that good"— what is that kind of good?—she said, "I'll deliver you a son," and we were ready, and he says, "Here, excuse me, I am in transit between births and smoke cigars to get the fetal fluid off my hands," and I said, "Great, Doc, just awful great, but be good and at your level best," and we ended up in a room that was just about as bad a room as you would ever want to be in, yeah, it was like a men's room, and everybody was all smiles, even Lisa, because it had crowned—my first look was peachfuzz on the cranium, damp as September rain, peeking through her mommie's opening, and at first I said, "No thank you," but the nurses are making me ashamed, they say the father is so important, and Lisa's saying, "We got up for this together so don't chicken on me, Jimmy," and I'm crying, thinking, whatever it is, it's alive, it's got wet hair on it. So I donned the blue suit and the blue booties and the blue mask and the blue hat and I waited, and I was saying, "James, you are a progenitor, and Lisa, you are the other thing"—I'm thinking, what's it, what's it, the progenetrix, and we neither of us know, we don't fuckin know, but we hope it works, and it was coming, man, was it ever coming, and then it got stuck: and there was panic everywhere except for Lisa, I mean, she didn't know, and the doctors looked at each other, back and forth, and they heated up the vacuum cleaners and the scalpels and they said, "Everybody, put your hands on her, altogether, and push, let's gather together and push," and this male doctor said "push," and this male intern said "push," and this male father said "push," and this male what-ever-the-hell-he-was said "push," and we helped her, we pushed while she pushed, and the only other woman in the room, who was the nurse, didn't push but listened with a stethoscope to see if it was alive, what we were pushing at and just like suddenly, one last push, and Bingo! a baby appeared, all covered completely in some shitstorm of cold-cream and tied by a cord to her mommy, and I said, "thanks," yeah, I said that, and it's likely more than thanks...and I noticed, well, I mean what can I say, yes, it was a little girl, right there, dressed in cream and a little poopy, stuck in the tubes like she was when I didn't even know the lady was a lady, and I thought only, not fuck off little person, you are not the man I wanted to come from there, I didn't think at all how bad my disappointment was. I didn't think anything, okay? Okay, I thought, just, you are my daughter and those people will wash the cream off you and in a while, I'm afraid, daughter, you'll be mine—and this is on a two-minute acquaintance in a delivery room—I thought, daughter, fuck it, from now till I die, I'll have to answer to you. When she popped out, whole and perfect, I mean, a little pooped, too long in the birth canal, all the light I ever had ran to her, all what I hoped, and in the bar around the corner from the hospital I told the keeper there, "I'm glad I didn't have a son," but what else could I say? *(Pause.)* What could I say? Somebody's got to tell *me. (Pause.)* I mean, did you ever think, Sergeant, when you saw your daughter the first time, that some part of you—was in her? Did you ever feel that, looking at Margie? Do you know what I mean? I mean, do you feel nothin at all, anyway at all, now she's dead? Say something!

Sally's Gone, She Left Her Name
by Russell Davis

The Play: The story of seventeen-year-old Sally Decker, her parents, Henry and Cynthia, and Christopher, her brother. Mom and Dad are not what they used to be, nor is the family; life is changing—nothing seems connected anymore.

Time and Place: Summer. The present. A large kitchen in a suburban home.

The Scene: Christopher confronts his father and his sister, Sally, who seems to have driven Mother out of the family.

• • •

CHRISTOPHER: You really screwed up, didn't you, Sally? You couldn't stay out of it, could you? I mean, I don't think it's any of our business what Mom and Dad do in their spare time. Just like they got to stay out of my spare time. I mean, as long as Dad uses his spare time to get into a good mood for around here, as long as he doesn't get nasty about it, I don't know, it's probably all right. But you had to step in, didn't you, Sally? Huh? Didn't you? And that's because you're jealous. You're jealous cause Mom's prettier than you'll ever be, and you're jealous Mom's got Dad, but as soon as Dad went and got anybody else, you couldn't stand it. *(Pause.)* You used to tell me a story, Dad. A real nice story about how Mom came from the next life we're supposed to live. Where people were better. Where they took care of each other better. You said our family was lucky. And it was your job to keep Mom away from knowing she was in the wrong life. You told me if you ever took your eyes off Mom, you'd turn around and she'd be gone. And you wouldn't know how. She could have just crumpled up, right in the air, and slipped away. That's why you married Mom. It was the best way you could figure to keep your eyes on her. And I used to ask you, can I help? And you said, sure, I could watch Mom too. *(Pause.)* I don't mind, it's probably all right, you couldn't keep doing it for eighteen years, keeping your eyes on Mom, and maybe she wanted to slip away somewhere anyway. But if you tell something like that, to a little kid, I was a little kid, you got to make it real. Otherwise you got no business telling it.

The Tempest

by William Shakespeare

The Play: Prospero, who was banished from power in Milan by his brother, the King of Naples, holds dominion over an enchanted island, where he eventually heals old wounds through his powers and brings about the marriage of his daughter, Miranda, to Ferdinand, the son of his enemy.

Time and Place: An enchanted island. Circa 1611.

The Scene: In the first speech (II, ii), the clown Trinculo, seeks shelter from an approaching storm after being shipwrecked on the island.

• • •

TRINCULO: Here's neither bush, no shrub to bear off any weather at all: and another storm brewing, I hear it sing i' th' wind: yond same black cloud, yond huge one, looks like a foul bombard, that would shed his liquor: if it should thunder, as it did before, I know not where to hide my head: yond same cloud cannot choose but fall by pailfuls. What have we here, a man, or a fish? dead or alive? A fish, he smells like a fish: a very ancient and fish-like smell: a kind of, not of the newest Poor-John: a strange fish: were I in England now (as once I was) and had but this fish painted, not a holiday fool there but would give a piece of silver: there, would this monster, make a man: any strange beast there makes a man: when they will not give a doit to relieve a lame beggar, they will lay out ten to see a dead Indian: legg'd like a man; and his fins like arms: warm o' my troth: I do now let loose my opinion; hold it no longer; this is no fish, but an islander, that hath lately suffered by a thunderbolt: alas, the storm is come again: my best way is to creep under his gaberdine: there is no other shelter hereabout: misery acquaints a man with strange bedfellows: I will here shroud till the dregs of the storm be past.

The Scene: *In the second speech (III, iii), Prosper's chief spirit, Ariel, casts a charm on his master's enemies.*

• • •

(Thunder and lightning. Enter Ariel (like a harpy) claps his wings upon the table, and with a quaint device the banquet vanishes.)

ARIEL: You are three men of sin, whom Destiny
That hath to instrument this lower world,
And what is in 't, the never-surfeited sea,
Hath caus'd to belch up you; and on this Island,
Where man doth not inhabit, you 'mongst men,
Being most unfit to live, I have made you mad;
And even with such-like valour, men hang, and drown
Their proper selves: you fools, I and my fellows
Are ministers of Fate; the elements
Of whom your swords are temper'd, may as well
Wound the loud winds, or with bemock'd-at stabs
Kill the still-closing waters, as diminish
One dowle that's in my plume; my fellow-ministers
Are like invulnerable: if you could hurt,
Your swords are now too massy for your strengths,
And will not be uplifted: but remember
(For that's my business to you) that you three
From Milan did supplant good Prospero,
Expos'd unto the sea (which hath requit it)
Him, and his innocent child: for which foul deed,
The Powers, delaying (not forgetting) have
Incens'd the seas, and shores: yea, all the creatures
Against your peace: thee of thy son, Alonso

They have bereft; and do pronounce by me
Lingering perdition (worse than any death
Can be at once) shall step by step attend
You, and your ways, whose wraths to guard you from,
Which here, in this most desolate Isle, else falls
Upon your heads, is nothing but heart's sorrow,
And a clear life ensuing.

Vieux Carre

by Tennessee Williams

The Play: "The Writer," a character in *Vieux Carre* fashioned after Mr. Williams, brings us into the world of a dilapidated rooming house in New Orleans' French Quarter. Part player and part narrator, The Writer reflects on the past by reliving that past. The collection of troubled souls that occupy the rooming house form a bizarre tapestry: a brash and desperate landlady, a well-bred young lady having a steamy relationship with a hot strip-joint worker, two older women clinging to the last remains of their dwindling income, a painter who is slowly dying, and our writer, struggling for purpose amidst conflicting feelings. A rich mix of humor, cruelty and poetry fuse together in the telling of this haunting story.

Time and Place: The period between winter 1938 and spring 1939. A rooming house in the French Quarter of New Orleans.

The Scene: The Writer (twenties) has confessed his sexual experience with a paratrooper to Nightingale, the ill painter who stays in the attic cubicle next to him. In the course of the scene, Nightingale has sympathized and then made his own sexual advance on The Writer. An hour later, in the reflection of the encounter, The Writer as narrator sits smoking on the foot of his cot, the sheet drawn about him like a toga. He speaks out front.

• • •

WRITER: When I was alone in the room, the visitor having retreated beyond the plywood partition between his cubicle and mine, which was chalk white that turned ash-gray at night, not just he but everything visible was gone except for the lighter gray of the alcove with its window over Toulouse

Street. An apparition came to me with the hypnotic effect of the painter's sandman special. It was in the form of an elderly female saint, of course. She materialized soundlessly. Her eyes fixed on me with a gentle questioning look which I came to remember as having belonged to my grandmother during her sieges of illness, when I used to go to her room and sit by her bed and want, so much, to say something or to put my hand over hers, but could do neither, knowing that if I did, I'd betray my feelings with tears that would trouble her more than her illness... Now it was she who stood next to my bed for a while. And as I drifted toward sleep, I wondered if she'd witnessed the encounter between the painter and me and what her attitude was toward such—perversions? Of longing?

(The sound of stifled coughing is heard across the plywood partition.)

WRITER: Nothing about her gave me any sign. The weightless hands clasping each other so loosely, the cool and believing gray eyes in the faint pearly face were as immobile as statuary. I felt that she neither blamed nor approved the encounter. No. Wait. She...seemed to lift one hand very, very slightly before my eyes closed with sleep. An almost invisible gesture of...forgiveness?...through understanding?...before she dissolved into sleep...

The Visible Horse

by Mary Lathrop

The Play: The two characters in Mary Lathrop's powerful play are Meg, a single mother, and Scott, her adolescent son. The father of this family has been dead a year, and Scott is having difficulty accepting his death. What begins as the bright solo insights of an intelligent and witty young teen, turns eventually into a profoundly moving acceptance and a deepening of the relationship between mother and son. Lathrop's convention is to balance monologues from Scott, with scenes between Meg and Scott, allowing us into the private thoughts of a young man refusing to accept the loss of his father and the struggles of a mother and son.

Time and Place: The present. The family condo, Scott's room, and Willow Lake of an unnamed city.

The Scene: It is Thursday afternoon. Scott with his bicycle. He takes a comb out of his pocket and combs his hair. He addresses the audience.

• • •

SCOTT: *(He takes a comb out of his pocket and combs his hair.)* I got a buzz. Buzzes are pretty cool. Only, see, I was gonna let my hair grow. I seen this picture of my dad when he was little, our age, and his hair waaaay long—man, it was awesome. I think he was a hippie or something. So I go, "Yo, Mom, I'm gonna grow my hair long, like that." And she goes, "Forget it. Nobody wears long hair anymore." Only when she takes me, we walk in, and the barber, right?, he has this hella long ponytail half ways down his back. For real! And I go, "So, Mom! Nobody's got long hair!" She was psyched out! And this hippie barber, he goes, "All the cool guys have buzzes." So I go, "Yeah? Guess you're not cool" Right? And my mom,

I thought she'd shit. I'm not kidding. And this barber goes, "I may not be cool, but I know what is cool. And buzzes are cool." No, he was way cool; he wouldn't take shit. So I go, "Okay." Right? Only when he cut it, this hippie barber, he gave me a bald spot, which I did not want. Anyways, I comb it back with gel, which smells good, and that's hygiene. Gel's way cool. Do you want to smell my buzz? *(He puts his comb back in his pocket.)*

The Scene: *It is Friday afternoon. Scott is wearing roller blades.*

• • •

SCOTT: 'Member that magic rock I showed you? Right? I mean, magic, hoo, they don't even do magic on TV—it's too fakey. Like McGuyver. McGuyver wouldn't ever do magic, right? McGuyver's way cool—scientific. Like each time he gets shit, which is every time—he has to or it wouldn't be interesting, right?—he doesn't wus out, cuz he knows chemistry and how to build bombs and that's science. This one time, McGuyver, he was locked up by these evil guys and he escaped by starting a fire with only a pocket mirror. Yeah! You really gotta know this stuff. And, heck, even little kids know you can start fires with mirrors. My dad, he showed me that a million years ago. A course, most guys don't carry mirrors, but now I do, because of McGuyver. *(He takes a mirror out of his pocket.)* Hey, I lucked out. I got it out of a gumball machine for twenty-five cents. You can't see yourself good, but it reflects fantastic. And you can start fires, and do signals, and such. *(He puts the mirror back in his pocket.)*

The Scene: *It is Monday afternoon. Scott stands on a skate-board.*

• • •

SCOTT: Sometimes I think I'm the model of the visible horse, like my guts are showing through my skin and they might read my mind, which I DO NOT WANT! Anyways, my teacher goes, "I've had about enough of you." You know the worst? I don't mind the office, I'm tough, but I had to sit there the rest of the day, cuz my mom couldn't come and get me. When she gets home, it's, like, all over. Because my mom, right?, she's already had enough grief for one lifetime. So like, "Yo, why'd you beeswax your teacher, Scott?" "Yo, Mom, because I was up all night with Dad, saying good-bye." You ever been sad and angry both at the same time? They both fit inside together. Right? Like, when my dad got wasted, I felt sad and angry. That makes sense. It does. But my mom, right?—I don't get it, I don't get it—she's sad, but kind of, like, happy, both. What is that? No, for real: I seen her do it at that lake. Sad and happy, crying, but smiling. Man, this is so weird. Oh! And I got to tell you this one other thing. And I'm not shitting you on this. Okay, we're in the middle of this lake in a rowboat, right? And my Mom opens up some wine, in honor of, like, my dad, right? And she hands the bottle to me! She goes, "Make a toast." I go, "Mother! You're breaking the law!" She goes, check this, she goes, "Go ahead, you can drink!" I'm not shitting. It was awesome.

159

160

CRAIG SLAIGHT is the Director of the Young Conservatory at American Conservatory Theater. As both a director and an acting teacher, Slaight has worked passionately to provide a creative and dynamic place for young people to learn and grow in theater arts. With a particular commitment to expanding the body of dramatic literature available to young people, Slaight has published seven anthologies with Smith and Kraus Publishers, *Great Scenes from the Stage for Young Actors,* and *Great Scenes for Young Actors Volume II, Great Monologues for Young Actors, Great Scenes and Monologues for Children, Multicultural Scenes for Young Actors, Multicultural Monologues for Young Actors,* and *Short Plays for Young Actors,* coedited by A.C.T.'s Jack Sharrar. *Great Monologues for Young Actors, Multicultural Monologues for Young Actors,* and *Multicultural Scenes for Young Actors* were selected by the New York Public Library as Outstanding Books for the Teenage. Additionally, Slaight created the New Plays Program at A.C.T.'s Young Conservatory in 1989 with the mission to develop plays by professional playwrights that view the world through the eyes of the young. The first nine New Plays are collected in Smith and Kraus Publisher's *New Plays from A.C.T.'s Young Conservatory, Volumes I and II. Volume II* also received recognition from the New York Public Library as an Outstanding Book for the Teenage in 1997. Educated in Michigan in Theater and English, Slaight taught at the junior and senior high school, college, and university levels, prior to moving to Los Angeles, where he spent ten years as a professional director (directing such notables as Julie Harris, Linda Purl, Betty Garrett, Harold Gould, Patrick Duffey, and Robert Foxworth). Slaight is currently a member of the Artistic Team at A.C.T. and frequently serves on the directing staff with the professional company. In addition to the work at A.C.T., Slaight is a consultant to the Educational Theater Association, the National Foundation for Advancement in the Arts, and is a frequent guest artist, speaker, workshop leader, and adjudicator for festivals and conferences throughout the country. In August of 1994, Slaight received the President's Award from The Educational Theater Association for outstanding contributions to youth theater. In January of 1998 Carey Perloff chose Slaight to receive the first annual A.C.T. Artistic Director's Award. Slaight makes his home in San Francisco, California.

JACK SHARRAR is Director of Academic Affairs for the American Conservatory Theater, where he serves on the MFA committee and teaches a variety of classes in the Young Conservatory. Dr. Sharrar is a graduate of the University of Michigan and holds a Ph.D. in theater history and dramatic literature from the University of Utah. His professional theater credits include roles at Michigan Repertory Theater, Mountainside Theater, the BoarsHead Theater, Theatre 40, Pioneer Theatre Company, and A.C.T. Studio. He has directed over 50 plays and musicals in secondary school, universities, and professional theaters, and is a member of Actors' Equity and the Screen Actor's Guild. He is author of *Avery Hopwood, His Life and Plays;* contributor to Oxford University Press's *The American National Biography;* and coeditor (with Craig Slaight) of *Great Scenes for Young Actors from the Stage, Great Monologues for Young Actors, Great Scenes and Monologues for Children, Multicultural Monologues for Young Actors, Multicultural Scenes for Young Actors,* and *Short Plays for Young Actors. Great Monologues for Young Actors, Multicultural Monologues for Young Actors,* and *Multicultural Scenes for Young Actors* were selected by the New York Public Library as Outstanding Books for the Teenage.